# RAISE YOUR GAME

Kate
Nurse

# RAISE YOUR GAME

## TIM RODBER

Hodder & Stoughton

Copyright © 1996 by Tim Rodber

First published in Great Britain in 1996 by
Hodder and Stoughton
a division of Hodder Headline PLC

10 9 8 7 6 5 4 3 2 1

A CIP catalogue record for this book is available
from the British Library.

ISBN 0 340 67232 3


Designed and typeset by
Penny Mills, Wrentham, Suffolk.

Printed and bound in Great Britain by
MacKays of Chatham.


Hodder and Stoughton Ltd
A division of Hodder Headline PLC
338 Euston Road
London NWI 3BH

# CONTENTS

# ACKNOWLEDGEMENTS

When I first contemplated writing this book I had no idea where to start — in fact the first few attempts were pretty awful. But eventually with the help of Roddy Bloomfield and all at Hodder & Stoughton I finally got things going.

My thanks to Ros Hargreaves who painstakingly translated my jumbled words into type and at the same time managed to make the best coffee in Northampton.

My biggest thank you goes to Phil Pask. His expertise and personal experiences in all fields of physical training and physiotherapy have been invaluable in the writing of this book. Not only has his professional help been excellent, but he has also been a very good friend over the past four years.

There are many people who have been involved in the development of my career but Ian McGeechan has been a constant source of inspiration to me. My thanks go to him and Northampton R.F.C. Ltd., a club that I first joined in 1988 and one which has been a home to me for the past eight years.

Finally my thanks to my parents and Jenny, my long suffering partner in crime, for all their encouragement and help over the years.

The author and publishers would like to thank Associated Sports Photography and Allsport for permission to reproduce their copyright photographs. The diagram on page 129 was drawn by Rodney Paull.

# YOUR ENGINEERS

For as long as I can remember I have grown up with sport. As a child, in the United States, from the ages of seven to eleven years old I played baseball, ice hockey, soccer, American football and basketball, to name but a few. I loved all sports and was never pressured by my parents to play sport or to follow one in particular, I simply enjoyed them all. I can't remember what my motivation was other than it was what everyone else was doing at the time. I guess I was extremely fortunate that every child played sports in America and that the opportunities were there for all children.

I never saw a rugby ball until I was eleven, when I started at Churcher's College in Petersfield, Hampshire. Rugby I thought was okay, but I preferred soccer and played for my local team until I was fifteen. Hockey and cricket were also on the agenda and enjoyed an equal footing with rugby, as it was a three-term sports school.

I played cricket, rugby and hockey at county level until I left school and then spent a year working in France before returning to attend a B.Sc. course in Human Biology at Oxford Brooke University. It was while at Oxford that my rugby began to blossom. I had represented the British Polytechnic XV and had caught the eye playing for the Army, who were sponsoring me through college. Barrie Corless, the newly appointed Director of Rugby at Northampton, spotted me and asked me to join the club. That started in 1989 my long association with the Saints.

It was during my second year at the club that Wayne Shelford arrived. He had enjoyed an undefeated run of 22 international matches as captain of New Zealand and had helped them win the Inaugural World Cup. He took it upon himself to become my personal tutor in the fine art of back-row play. There is no doubt in my mind that his influence considerably accelerated my promotion to the England ranks, so effectively that the 1992 Five Nations Championship saw a new number eight represent England against Scotland.

So there I was, with only three years' experience at senior level, raw to say the least, playing at Murrayfield. I was catapulted into the world of international competition that for years had been a notoriously hard school of knocks, and into a team that was well established and the previous year had won the Grand Slam. On top of all that I was replacing one of rugby's great players, Dean Richards. It was a nerve-wracking experience, but at the time I was confident that I would be able to cope with it.

After a very indifferent 55 minutes I suffered a serious neck injury. I had tackled Kenny Milne from a line-out, swung round, and the top of my head made contact with Jason Leonard's hip. I was spinally concussed, an injury which resulted in temporary paralysis and massive compression of the neck. It was the most frightening moment of my life.

I lost control of my body. There was a huge rushing of pins and needles and I fell to the ground and turned my head towards the touch line. Kevin Murphy, the massively experienced England and British Lions physiotherapist, immediately ran on.

'I can't feel anything, Smurf.'

In his immensely calming and reassuring way he said, 'Oh shit!'

Fortunately for me, as soon as I had said it, the pins and needles subsided and slowly the feeling returned to my feet, arms and body. I did walk off the field, and in fact attended the post-match dinner. It had not been the best of starts to my international career and I hadn't gained any respect from the other players for leaving the field. On the Monday morning I returned to the Royal Military Academy, Sandhurst, where I had just started my Army officer training. I was still suffering from pins and needles in my shoulders, cold sweats, headaches and a total loss of feeling in both hands. Rather foolishly, in hindsight, I was determined to be fit for the next match against Ireland. I did play in the game, performing better than against Scotland, but I was dropped and then sat on the bench for the remaining games and consequently for the whole of the 1993 Championship as well.

At the time of getting my first cap I weighed sixteen and a half stone, was six foot six inches tall and had a sixteen-and-a-half-inch neck. I was an aerobically fit and talented player, reasonably quick for someone so tall, who enjoyed the social side of rugby as much as the playing, if not more. At the top level I was found wanting. Not physically big enough and

certainly nowhere near mentally tough enough. It was these factors and my injury that made me determined to do something about it. Whenever I was to be given another chance I would be ready ... ready to make sure I played well, did myself justice and this time kept my place.

At nineteen years old and physically inferior, as Mick 'the Munch' Skinner is about to prove.

It was at that stage in 1992 that my close friend and mentor, and now co-author, Phil Pask, took me under his wing. We sat down together and designed the training programme that would propel me back into the England team.

Phil's credentials speak for themselves. He obtained a degree in Physical Education from Birmingham University, where his appetite for sport was fuelled and he began to play rugby and judo, a lethal combination. He excelled in judo, winning the North of England Championships in 1980, and spent many years training with players such as Brian Jacks, David Starbrook and Neil Adams. From there, not happy with the heights he had scaled in judo, he took up triathlon, completing twenty-seven, including the world championships, the Hawaiian Iron Man. He had been playing rugby for fun, but decided to take it seriously. He joined Northampton and had a successful career, playing in the Pilkington Cup final and the

Typical! Phil Pask is the only man I know to smile at the end of the gruelling Three Peaks race.

Middlesex Sevens, winning the Second Division title and finally, in 1994, representing England in the Paris Sevens Tournament.

As his rugby flourished he opted for a change of career and attended the Queen Elizabeth School of Physiotherapy. He is now in private practice as a physiotherapist in Northampton. Phil's broad experiences of sport at every level mean that he has knowledge of the specific fitness requirements that are needed for a first-class rugby player.

He is not a trainer who stands, whistle in hand, encouraging and criticising. In the three years since we first sat down in the planning stages, we are still training together, pushing each other, trying to get one up on the other, every time we train, every day of the week.

In writing this book, we felt that it was not just to be about rugby or any particular sport as such. My story is just one of millions of other sportsmen and women throughout the world. I was someone who never had the right training programme, neither physically nor mentally, to advance my initial ability. There is no doubt in my mind, had I not undertaken to change my fitness lifestyle, I would not have played for England again.

This book is aimed at sportsmen and women of all ages and abilities who wish to improve themselves physically, so that they either achieve more in their chosen sport or simply get themselves fitter.

Alongside the physical aspect will of course run the mental side, dealing with the development of your own sports mind. What we are saying is not the be-all and end-all, it is just our personal experiences related in a simple way with input from other sporting personalities.

# CHAPTER 1:

# THE ENGINE AND THE CHASSIS

I totally despised training when I was first capped for England. I was still in student mode then, though I had just started to take life seriously as I had begun the intensive eight-month Army Officer Training Course at the Royal Military Academy, Sandhurst. Until that point training, and specific training in particular for rugby, was, in my eyes, boring. However, Sandhurst helped to ensure that I would appreciate the need for specific fitness training.

Once I had left Sandhurst and started to take rugby seriously, Phil and I got together. It was all well and good sitting there with Phil at the beginning with the best of intentions about starting afresh, but at that stage actually getting up and doing something about it was the sort of stuff nightmares are made of. I can remember our first training session together: it was bloody awful. A fartlek run during which I was physically sick, followed by circuit training in the gym where my muscles burned so much I was convinced I was doing more harm than good: he nearly killed me.

I know now in hindsight that it was his way of breaking the ice, shutting out the cocky young rugby player that I was, breaking me down into something he could then build back up again. However, as is often the case when you start something new and don't enjoy it at first, my attitude was poor. I was slow to take to Phil and his methods and occasionally I was even known not to turn up to training.

Looking back, I am not sure whether this was because of fear of not completing the exercise, or of actual fear of Phil himself. All the same, eventually I started to appreciate what we were doing and the results started to show on the rugby field.

It has always surprised me how much respect is paid to an

individual who is physically fit. You must have seen it yourselves wherever you go – if you are at a sports meeting, athletics track, rugby match, even around the golf course, people who talk of sport always marvel how fit or how fast or how strong individuals are. In my case it was no different: I was amazed as to how fit Phil was and he constantly annoyed me with his ability to run alongside me and talk to me all the time while I would be sweating through every pore on my body. Eventually, Phil's superior fitness brought out the naturally competitive edge that was hiding within me and I was determined that one day it would be me that was pushing him. I am still waiting for that day to come.

Over the years my eyes have slowly been opened to the need for a specific structured training programme that is relevant to the needs of the sport that you play. Those of the more astute of you will wonder why an individual with a degree in Human Biology hadn't already realised that there was a need to put the theory of physical fitness, and mental fitness, into practice. For some obscure reason I had never really applied any of the theory to myself. I guess when I was a student, and in my early days of training with Phil, I suffered from that old classic of having no one to train with and so I was never really pushed into training. I also, as you must have found yourselves, used to stick to the sort of training that I was good at and that I found easy.

This, of course, is not a good thing. For years I had arms like Garth but the chest of Davey Jones' locker – sunken. Finding someone to train with is something so simple that it is without doubt golden rule number one. It is best to find someone who is fitter than you, who is happy to push you to your limits, to be patient with you and, of course, to make you feel guilty when you don't particularly feel like training, or when you don't even turn up. As you get further down the line you can start training in groups. Group training can be a great motivator.

The word 'fitness' can be defined in many ways, and in every type of sport every type of person has his own idea of the definition of physical fitness. As far as Phil and I are concerned it is important that everybody understands what fitness is all about, not just the word and not just the image, but a bit of the biology of it, because that will make you understand why you are doing something. When you're flogging your guts out on a Friday night in the rain when there are a couple of beers waiting for you in a warm bar, there is nothing worse than to think you are doing it for nothing. If you can understand why, that often helps you.

In our minds there are eight components to a sports person that will contribute to his or her performance in any chosen sport. These are:

1) cardiovascular or aerobic endurance
2) anaerobic endurance
3) strength
4) speed
5) flexibility
6) body composition, i.e. diet and nutrition
7) skill, i.e. agility, co-ordination and balance
8) psychological approach

All of these are equally important, though in some sports, such as long-distance running, body strength is obviously not as important as cardiovascular aerobic endurance. As far as rugby is concerned, it is one of the few games where an individual must have the aerobic endurance to run for 80 minutes and the anaerobic endurance to carry out repeated sprints, and must be strong enough in the upper body to withstand the tackling and the physical confrontation. His body composition, i.e. diet and fat content, must be well monitored to enhance performance, his skill must be top quality so that he can play the game; and of course his mental approach must be first class so that he can compete at a high level. Rugby in fact is one of the few sports that draws on every part of physical fitness to contribute to a high performance.

## CARDIOVASCULAR AEROBIC ENDURANCE

This is without doubt one of the hardest parts of fitness training. It basically determines how far an individual can run; the greater his aerobic endurance the further he can run for a longer period of time. Within the England rugby set-up over the last ten years this has been the part of training that the England fitness experts considered needed improvement. Consequently, our training involved endless amounts of long-distance running, biking and swimming. This is still the case in many ways, although now the emphasis is more on speed and power, so the training schedules have changed. The 1995 Rugby World Cup and Jonah Lomu of New Zealand proved that stamina is definitely not everything. Jonah Lomu was renowned for being a bad trainer. The New Zealanders used to do a three-mile run every Sunday morning to get rid of the lactic acid that had built up the previous day. Jonah always came last – he was even beaten by their coach Laurie Maines who was in his fifties. He was of course given hell for it, but on the rugby field Jonah Lomu, as everyone will have seen, is one of the biggest, strongest and most powerful runners in the world of rugby. He can run 100 metres in under 11 seconds. He is $19\frac{1}{2}$ stone in weight and six feet five inches tall. If he were to play in the back row, instead of the wing, however, he would need a change of emphasis to his fitness training.

There are, of course, certain individuals when it comes to aerobic training and aerobic endurance who are in a class of their own. There are several within the England squad. My friend Ian Hunter, who plays at Northampton, has a natural ability and a naturally high $VO_2$ – which is shorthand for the body's capacity to consume oxygen. He can run what is known as the bleep test (repeated 20-metre shuttle runs) up to level 15.10 – at $15\frac{1}{2}$ stone this is not an easy feat.

On the other hand, Alan Buzza has been known to get to level 17 of the $VO_2$ max test (which discovers the maximum rate at which you can consume oxygen), but he is a whippet, about $13\frac{1}{2}$ stone. After I'd got to level 12.8 and he had reached 17 at one particularly enjoyable England fitness testing session at Twickenham, I asked him what training methods he used to get such a high level, expecting some kind of enlightening answer. He said he did no specific training for endurance. This I couldn't believe and hardly do to this day. But it is true that there is a genetic link between $VO_2$ max and genes, and it is worth noting that Alan Buzza's brother has run for Great Britain, not in the 100 metres, but in the marathon.

I have never been particularly good in this area. At 18 stone and six feet six inches I have always found running long distances gave my joints, especially my back and knees, a lot of problems, and as you will see later my training is specifically designed to help me avoid putting undue stress on these joints. I was not alone within the England squad. Victor Obogu, the powerful prop, used to hate the $VO_2$ max test, and a great friend of mine Allan Lamb the cricketer, also detested it. It is, without doubt, one of the hardest tests to do, not so much physically but mentally. You are forever reaching brick walls so you stop and then one minute later you are ready to go again, but by then it is too late. Aerobic fitness is the backbone of all sports; you must be aerobically fit. To play rugby you don't have to be a marathon runner and you don't have to be Linford Christie, but to be a good player you need a combination of the two.

## ANAEROBIC ENDURANCE

This is best reflected by looking at the job of a back-row forward in a game of rugby. The back-row forward, along with the scrum-half, is likely to work nearly 100 per cent of the time he is on the field. Anaerobic endurance is the ability to perform at a high sustained rate, perhaps 80 to 95 per cent of maximum effort followed by a short rest, then repeating the activity again and again and again. Once you are above three minutes you enter a realm of aerobic endurance; up to three minutes is anaerobic endurance. To achieve better anaerobic endurance you will need plenty of interval training and fartlek running, 300 metres on the track, 50 metres on the track, repeated sprints. These tend to be the gut wrenchers – the ones that make you sick because your heart is working at a very high rate, near to its maximum for relatively long periods of time, and is then given a short period of rest to recover before it is made to work again. Often this tough training is known as the 'sickeners' (gut wrenchers).

Extreme anaerobic ability was the target sought by the judo champions Dave Starbrook and Brian Jacks, who as part of their international training would perform a series of shuttles across the mat in the dojo. These two would delight in going as fast as possible for as long as possible – until one of them dropped. Starbrook was determined to get his heart rate higher than the squad doctors thought possible!

It is important to note that running is neither aerobic nor anaerobic, but a blend of the two depending on the intensity and duration of the activity.

## STRENGTH

Strength training for sport does not mean you have to look like Arnold Schwarzenegger overnight and it most certainly doesn't mean that you take any kind of stimulants to increase your muscle development. People who dabble in anabolic

1988 Olympics – the combination of strength, speed, agility and above all determination.

steroids obviously don't understand the type of side effects that they bring – and the simple fact is that to touch them is to cheat.

Strength plays an integral part in rugby when making tackles, scrummaging and ripping the ball off an opponent. Being physically strong enough to tackle an individual and knock him backwards is the ultimate aim of strength training in rugby. It varies in its type. A prop forward will tend to do a lot of pure strength training in the gym; a back, in general, will tend to work on lighter weights so that although he will not be as strong as a prop, he will be physically fitter. Jason Leonard, or 'The Bus' as we call him, is one of the strongest

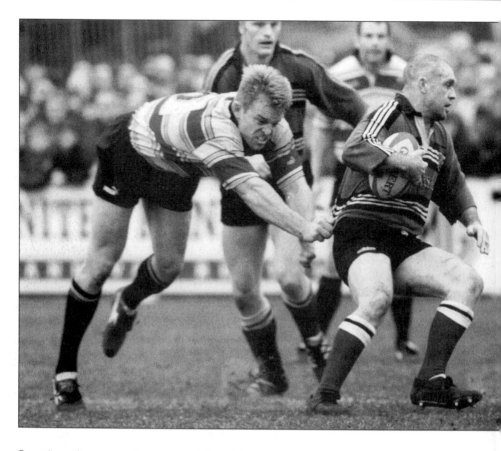

Sometimes the shirt-tail is the only option.

(Opposite) Paul Grayson (Northampton and England) demonstrates good sprinting technique.

rugby players that I know. Only years of experience and hard work in the gym has got him where he is now.

Remember: it is not how big you are, but how strong you are that matters.

## SPEED

Talk of speed and you will think of Linford Christie. In terms of fitness, speed is an integral part of most games. Speed training obviously involves repeated sprints, but it does also involve a lot of gym work and a lot of power training to increase the type of muscle that you need for speed. I have always enjoyed doing sprint training and power work in the gym, but I've had my ups and downs. In 1993, when doing some sprint training with my England colleague, Matt Dawson and my England Sevens colleague Nick Beal, things went horribly wrong.

We were doing some over-runs, (approximately 125-metre runs) on the back pitch at Northampton. Obviously, when you

train together things get competitive and on this occasion it was no different. We had decided to sprint for beer. Whoever lost the sprints would pay for the beer, and being a wily old fox and the only forward of the three of us, I decided to cheat. I jumped the gun and got a five-metre start on both of them. As I was cruising past the halfway line Nick Beal cruised past me, but there was no sign of Matt. As we approached the 22 and a particularly muddy part of the pitch, for some reason I fell over. Dawson, laughing and joking, went past me and won, claiming a pint. To his horror, and most certainly to mine, I'd injured my knee in the fall. At that point I had no idea why I'd fallen, but when Matt saw the cut on my knee, some four inches long and down to the bone, it suddenly became obvious to me, as he turned a whiter shade of pale, that it was his fault that I'd fallen. He was later to tell me he had dived and tap-tackled me in the mud, sending me down. The result of all this was twenty-seven stitches in my left knee: it wasn't the best sprint-training session I'd ever done!

In rugby terms, when you think of speed you immediately think of people like Rory Underwood and Martin Offiah. I can remember when Wigan announced to the rugby-loving public that there would be a sprint challenge at Central Park in Wigan. Rory Underwood was asked to represent the Rugby Union contingent. However, he couldn't and Steve Hackney, the Leicester wing who was renowned for being very, very quick, took up the challenge of racing against Offiah. At that time Steve was quite confident. He had been sprint training for many months and he was a sub-11 second man; however, as he tells the story, by the time he got out of the blocks he could read the label on the back of Offiah's shorts. It was incredible. Martin Offiah is without doubt one of the quickest rugby players in the world and his scuttling running style has not held him back.

## FLEXIBILITY

The word flexibility seems to turn people off. Everyone I know, whether he or she plays sport or not, thinks that flexibility is unimportant; thinks it is the last thing they should concentrate on and thinks that it is better to get on with the exercise than to do any stretching. Well, nothing could be further from the truth.

We cannot place enough importance on warming up and warming down, with a good routine of stretches that incorporates all the major muscle groups within the body. Not only does it prevent injury by warming up the muscles sufficiently to take part in exercise, but it also enables the lengthening of the muscles which can allow a greater range of movement, helping the running action of an individual. The more flexible you are, inevitably the higher knee lifts you can get and so the bigger stride you can get. To your surprise I am sure, the most flexible people within the England team are the front row. Sometimes it is the backs who are the most inflexible in the team. Gary Pearce, the former England prop, is one of the most flexible people I have ever met. There has been many a time when I have played second-row behind him, and in the middle of the scrum he has been looking at me face to face through his legs, holding up the whole scrum on the small of his back and his neck. That is not something you should try at home, but it can be done and it is regularly done by many props throughout the country. I wouldn't like to see Gary's body when he's fifty.

Flexibility is fine, but not up to the point of hypermobility – too much range of movement in a joint can lead to injury. This type of joint needs strong muscle around to support it.

## BODY COMPOSITION

Again, this is often an area that many people pass by. Body composition, diet, nutrition, are areas that need to be taken into account when looking at a definition of physical fitness. The lifestyle that an individual leads will dictate ultimately how fit he or she will get. If you go out every night and have a few pints and a couple of cigarettes, I'm afraid you'll put weight on and you will do yourself no good at all. If you have one blow-out a week on a Saturday night and perhaps a social cigarette, but the rest of the time you monitor what you eat and what you drink; if you keep off the red meat as a rule, perhaps eating it once a week, if you have a low-fat diet, no fry-ups, no fried eggs, grill everything, and eat plenty of fresh fruit and vegetables, then ultimately that will help your fitness training programme and underline it as you develop into a fitter person. This area sees the downfall of many. The temptation of going out for a drink, or if you are sitting at home on an evening eating chocolate or crisps, is something we have all been through. Everyone has their foibles. Most people enjoy the odd pint, the odd bag of biscuits, but in the long run if you can curb such indiscretions it will help you along the way towards your goal to become a fitter person. A balanced diet and everything in moderation is probably the best way forward.

Mick Skinner used to call anyone who was overweight a fat boy and he was quite happy to tell them so. At the end of the day, if you put weight on, people see; if you are happy with it then so be it, but if you can take up the challenge of trying to change your lifestyle and become a fitter person and develop your own sporting talents, then being called a fat boy is the ultimate degradation. By the way, Skinner wasn't so thin himself. We should all remember it's actually hard work carrying a 24lb 'bag of spuds' around a 400-metre track or attempting 15 pull-ups with it on your back.

## SKILL

Of course, to play a sport you must have a certain amount of skill. Running, the balance of it, co-ordination, etc., all come into play. Jerry Guscott is one of the most skilful people I have ever seen. He can kick with both feet, he is a beautifully balanced runner with tremendous pace, he has a high aerobic endurance, he is strong and he has great hands in the pass; and his skills can also be seen in his tennis and golf. Skills can be learned and developed over the years, but most people have the basics in there naturally.

It is most important in my opinion to develop your skills, not by just playing your chosen sport, but by playing other sports. When I was at school I played rugby, hockey and cricket. enjoyed my tennis and squash, I was a keen golfer and even took part in activities like skiing and water sports. All of these undoubtedly have contributed to my skill levels, and even now, although I have little time for other sports, I always try to play tennis and golf in summer and I enjoy the odd game of cricket as well. Cross-training can add a bit of variety to your schedule and help with motivation too.

## MENTAL

The last part of our definition of physical fitness is the psychological, or mental, approach. This is often the difference between winning and losing, achieving or not achieving. Motivating yourself and overcoming your fears and nerves

)eing able to cope with the pressures of training is not easy.
3ut if you are mentally and psychologically fit you will be able
.o cope with it and that will undoubtedly help you as a
sportsperson.

## POSITIVE THINKING

Positive thinking is something you've often heard of and probably never really understood. Use of positive thoughts, positive memories; experiences that have been good, successful, made you feel good in the past, are what this is all about. To achieve that goal, whether it's in training, during a game, running 400 metres the fastest or pushing the heaviest weight, the use of positive thinking is essential. Belief in yourself is essential. Belief in yourself is everything. So how do you use it? Well, it is very simple.

In your mind, before you undertake an event you have to have a positive outlook: you have to believe in yourself, in what you're doing and why you are doing it. To help you do that you need to refer to positive memories that you have had in the past: for example, I use the memory of making the final in the 1993 World Cup Sevens. When I am finding a training session particularly hard I will focus on a past experience like winning the World Cup Final or focus on a future experience and look at it positively and use it to motivate me to drive myself on. The use of replaying positive experiences in your training is the first step towards using mental rehearsal and trigger experiences, as I call them, whereby during a game, an event, or a particular training session, you can use a particular experience as a motivational tool. An individual word, for instance, can be used. If I am thinking of the World Cup Sevens when I scored a try running the length past David Campese, I might use the word 'Campese' and think of that memory when I am finding training particularly tough. The same applies for future events. If I am three weeks away from the beginning of the Five Nations and I am training and finding it tough, I will use that forthcoming match at the back of my mind to drive me on. For you it's a learning process. Work out what sticks in your mind as a positive memory, or a positive thought and replay it over and over again. Use it as a trigger to motivate you during hard sessions.

Nick Faldo consistently reaps the benefits through concentration and positive thinking.

The big question is 'Are you tough enough to start a train ing programme, however modest it may be?' Never mind, fol low it through. The hardest part is starting and what you nee to help you is a bit of positive thinking.

# CHAPTER 2

# ON THE ROAD

## WORLD CUP SEVENS

No mental and physical effort in sport could be much greater than that expended by the young England side who won the World Cup Sevens tournament in 1993, and the memory of that rugby success will stay with me for the rest of my life. It was, and will remain, an important lesson to all of us in sport, at whatever level: no matter what other people think of your chances, through hard work, good leadership and intense determination you can succeed. That is why the story of that triumph is worth telling here.

About four weeks before that tournament – the first World Cup for Rugby Sevens ever held – I received a letter from the Rugby Football Union asking me to take part. Four weeks away from a major tournament and we had had no preparation. While most of the other sides taking part had been playing in various parts of the world, we had not played in any Sevens tournaments at all. We were underrated by the RFU and basically given no hope. Far from the team being selected from the England XV, I was the only player who was involved within the full national squad.

We all assembled at the Bank of England ground at Roehampton two weeks before the tournament on a cold and wet weekend. We were thrown together: myself, Andy Harriman, the captain, Damian Hopley, Lawrence Dallaglio, Chris Sheasby, Justyn Cassell, Matt Dawson, Dave Sculley, Nick Beal and Adedayo Adebayo. 'Thrown together' was the phrase because, as I said, we were given no hope. Peter Rossborough was the manager and Les Cusworth the coach, backed up with a medical team of Barney Kenny and Dr Paul Jackson. We had no idea how successful we would be – whether we would be a flop and an embarrassment, or achieve the highest honour. When any team has had no preparation and is not rated by anyone, the press – or even your own selectors – can cause major stress and worry. However, we were young and we were ambitious. Andy Harriman was an excellent captain and in Cusworth and Rossborough we had a fine management team, so rather than be negative about the whole situation, the team accepted being underdogs and had the attitude that we didn't care what anyone said, we were just going to go out, play for each other, play for ourselves and enjoy it.

Harriman, who achieved one cap for England in the late 'eighties against Australia, was well respected by all the team. He was a superb Sevens player with blinding natural pace, and he got it right in the build-up. He wasn't too strict, he wasn't too worried about discipline, he was merely worried about getting the other nine players in the right frame of mind so that they were full of passion and desire when they put on the shirt of England in this tournament. It was to be one of the most physically and mentally draining seven days of my rugby career.

We travelled up to Murrayfield the week before the tournament started, and arrived late on the Sunday night at our hotel, the George, in the heart of Edinburgh. We had seven days to train, to prepare, to organise ourselves, to get ourselves mentally and physically in the right condition to play the world's best teams in the most important rugby tournament in the Sevens calendar.

The training started fairly well. We were abrasive with each other and started to get a bit of team feeling going. Our defence was looking very strong and we decided that with Andy Harriman as our finisher, and our defence as the backbone of the team, we could do well. Three days later we took on a local club side and they beat us. There we were, written off by everyone, and sure enough we lose in a practice match to a local Scottish club side – enough to cause most people to crumple. Even the Scottish bag men appointed to look after our kit were shaking their heads in disbelief. But still we were confident.

It was at about this stage on the Wednesday, two days before the tournament started, that Peter Rossborough began to talk about mental rehearsal and visualisation techniques during the team meetings in the evenings. We would sit in a cramped room and talk for half an hour about what we were going to try and achieve; about the physical and mental pressures that we would overcome in each game of Sevens. He would try to help us go through mental rehearsal so that we would rehearse in our own minds, our own jobs during a game. We would rehearse the first scrum, the first line-out, the first tackle, the first pass. We would rehearse all the positive things that needed to be thought about. We didn't think about losing the ball. We didn't think about dropping a pass. We thought about the positive aspects: beating a man on the outside; making a big tackle; winning the line-out; winning a kick-off; scoring a try. These mental rehearsal techniques carried on through Thursday into Friday and into the tournament itself and they were the backbone of the team's inner confidence and belief in themselves.

The tournament started on Friday and went through until Sunday. Each match was a learning process. While the other teams already knew which moves worked and who was playing well, we had to work it out on the Friday and Saturday. Eventually we qualified for the final day in a group with New Zealand, South Africa and Australia.

One of the most notable aspects of the weekend was the reception that the team got from the Murrayfield crowd. Every time we ran out, we were booed. That could have put pressure on the young players, it could have meant mistakes, it could have meant us losing. Instead it fuelled the fire. It inspired every player and it brought the best out of them.

The nationalism that we felt in the team as England was immense. We did not want to stand down and lose for one second. Our body language when we went on the field was superb. We knew if we went out there, heads down, slumped shoulders, the crowd for one would know they were getting to us and the opposition would think, 'We've got this.' Our chests were out, shoulders were back and we wore the English Rose with pride.

We had a monumental task on that Sunday: New Zealand at 10 o'clock in the morning, South Africa at 11.30 and then Australia at 1.00, and if we got through all of that we had a semi-final and final to play. This was to be the moment of truth. We were up there with the big boys; could we survive? Could we do it?

The New Zealand match was one of the best games I have ever played. The team was so highly motivated, every tackle that was made resulted in the New Zealanders dropping the ball or losing possession. It was intense from minute one to minute fourteen. The ferocity of that game set the stall out for the rest of the day.

Against South Africa it was a very tough and torrid battle too, but we got through, and that meant we had qualified. We played Australia and lost.

At this stage there were a few worries creeping in. Damian Hopley, who'd played well so far, had a calf injury and was ruled out of the tournament. We had to take a player from a Scottish pool of replacements and that was Michael Dods. He is a Scotsman through and through, but he's a team man, a team player, and his character and personality endeared him to the rest of the team and ensured that he played a vital role in the winning of the World Cup.

The semi-final was against Fiji. Fiji have, without doubt, the best Sevens players in the world. They have consistently won tournaments worldwide and are very highly rated, but unfortunately for them, it was a damp afternoon at Murrayfield and there were seven Englishmen ready to provide the upset of the year. We had nothing to lose, we were the underdogs all the way through.

World champions!

But we had a mission, and the mission was to win. We did so, fairly convincingly, and so the stage was set for the World Cup Final – England against Australia.

## MOTIVATION

This is the key to everything. Why have you picked up the book? Why have you decided to get fit? What are your reasons, positive and negative? What are your fears? All these factors need to be analysed in your own mind. Some people find getting motivated easy. They just understand that they have to be positive, have to go out and achieve these goals. Others find it difficult to motivate themselves, they struggle to achieve the goals they set themselves because they don't understand why they started in the first place. Setting yourself a target is what it's all about, and setting yourself an achievable one is just as important. Don't pick up this book expecting to be Sebastian Coe in three weeks – it won't happen. Set yourself a realistic target, a realistic challenge, weighed up by the parameters that affect your life – time off, for example. You will find that once you achieve this goal then others will come more easily. The motivation to succeed has got to come from yourself but can be helped by a training partner or someone close to you, such as your spouse. Losing weight need not necessarily be a motivational factor, but it can be one of many. Losing weight, getting fitter, getting stronger so that you can play a better standard of sport is the real motivation. If you need your girlfriend or wife to help and encourage you, egg you on, then tell them: explain to them that you need the encouragement. If you need a training partner – which I thoroughly recommend – then get one and get one who is highly motivated himself. Someone who is prepared to put pressure on you to make you feel guilty, to pick you up when you are down and to sometimes knock you down when you are up!

However, at the end of the day your motivation must come from yourself. You cannot blame anyone else. You cannot look for excuses. The success of an individual, whether it is in sport, business or family life, comes down to the individual himself, not because of some extraneous circumstance. You cannot blame anything on anyone else. It is up to you. Work out what you need to do, set yourself realistic goals and achieve them. If you're not sure why you're doing it, sit down on your own for an hour and write down your reasons for what you are trying to achieve; why you are trying to do it. You'll soon find that you have a long list of good reasons, and ones that can be referred to when the motivation on a cold wet day isn't quite there.

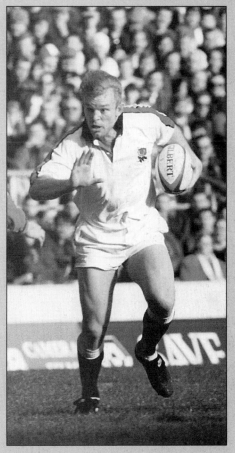

Putting on the red rose of England is my greatest motivation.

We had already lost to Australia, but we knew that we could beat them. Tactically we were switched on and our desire and our motivation was greater than theirs. We were tired and we were carrying injuries; it had been a long, hard week, but we wanted it. Three tries were scored in the first six minutes and from then we hung on, playing with the passion that the shirt warrants. Australia must have thought that there were ten Englishmen on the field that day. We walked out of the stadium World Champions.

We achieved something that very few people ever get near to and we'd done it without anyone rating us, without any backing, without preparation. We won because we had the will to win, great teamwork and camaraderie that was felt throughout the squad and the management. It was one of the best moments of my rugby career and I shall never forget it.

## THE NORTHAMPTON WAY

The season of 1994–5 started in the worst possible way for Northampton Rugby Club. The Saints, of which I was captain, began their league campaign without a single win in eight games. Ian McGeechan, their new coach, arrived at that point in the season, mid-November. From then on he began to improve and alter the way we were playing. Unfortunately, it was too late. We were relegated that year.

We had been promoted to the first division in 1989 and worked very hard throughout to maintain the standards, but for the first time since then we had succeeded in ruining what could have been a good season. It wasn't through lack of high ability either. The likes of myself, Martin Bayfield, Matt Dawson, Paul Grayson, Ian Hunter and Peter Walton were all international players, but all relatively young and inexperienced. During the season injuries to key players, and also the demands of that year due to the World Cup, all contributed to making the Northampton Saints' year a miserable one.

However, towards the end of that year we started to turn the corner. Ian McGeechan's coaching policies had begun to infiltrate the team and we ended the season with four wins on the trot.

Towards the end of it, Ian McGeechan, Phil Pask (who was the club's fitness adviser and coach) and I sat down and tried to establish where we were going, what we were trying to do, and how we were going to try and achieve it. We knew we were relegated. We knew we had to face a year in the second division, but rather than take that in a negative way, we decided that we would use it positively. We decided that we would set out a battle plan and we worked our goals out, long term, intermediate and immediate.

Our longterm goal of course was to get back into division one. Coupled with that we wanted to play a certain style and brand of rugby that would be memorable to both ourselves and the fans, and at the end of the day would make a statement to everyone in the first and second divisions that we were coming back into the top flight.

Our intermediate goals for that year, that were set out to try and achieve our long-range goals, were to improve the fitness of the team and to improve the basic knowledge of the game plan that we were trying to instil.

Our short-term goals, which changed rapidly throughout the year, basically concerned fitness and style of play. In terms of fitness we knew we had to work harder: we knew we had to increase our 'runability', our strength and our power, and we set about this during pre-season: hard training at high intensity for long periods, to the point of being sick in some cases. With this base of fitness we knew that we could play the style of rugby that we wanted to play. Getting the players to understand that style began in the coaching sessions, and each time we trained we put new skills into the practices, so that slowly the team and the players built up the picture they needed to produce the style of play we wanted.

This process of goal-setting, working from our longterm goals, then working out our consequent intermediate goals and taking from them the various short-term goals and achieving them, became an essential part in the development of Northampton Rugby Club. It enabled Ian, Phil and me to build up a picture of where we were trying to go with the team, how each individual was progressing and how he would react and respond to the challenge of the style of play and the fitness training that we would lay down.

Having achieved our immediate fitness goals, we set about the season in dramatic style. The way we tried to play was a quick, expansive, 15-man game at 100 miles an hour, working for 80 minutes. It was a tall order and certainly when we were 15–0 down after ten minutes in our first game against London Irish there was a certain amount of negativity creeping into the side. However, the confidence that the pre-

## MENTAL REHEARSAL

You may have heard the story of David Hemery, the 400-metre hurdler. He rehearsed mentally before the Olympic final that he would finish in first place. He went through the whole process, crossing each hurdle, running each step crossing that line ahead, until in the end he achieved his goal and won the race. He said afterwards it was purely down to the fact that he had rehearsed it so many times, it became the natural thing to do. He believed he couldn't lose. Again, the use of positive experiences is essential.

Before a big game my mental rehearsal will begin three or four days beforehand. During International week while in team meetings I will rehearse in my own mind how I am going to play, what I am going to try and achieve in the game, and as the days get closer to the match it is all finally honed. About two hours before kick-off, I will sit in a bath in my hotel room with the TV and radio switched off and the door closed and I will relax. It is here that I go through my final mental rehearsal and preparation for the game. I will go through in my mind the first tackle, the first catch, the first line-out, the first scrum and the role that I play in each of those. I will use positive events from the past to refer to, so that by the time I get out of the bath fifteen minutes later, my mind is totally focused and ready for the challenge of the first tackle, the first pass, etc.

This mental rehearsal is very important and key to the success of any athlete in any sport. You can even use it during training. Before training starts use the positive thoughts of the past and imagine yourself doing well during that training session over and over again. Project yourself forward if you like, into a state where you are achieving your goals. Use the positive thinking that you already know together with mental rehearsal and you will achieve all your training and match goals.

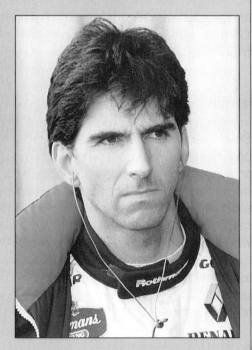

Damon Hill totally focused before a big race.

season fitness training had instilled in everyone ensured that we were going to keep working at the style of play we wanted. The game ended 69–31 to Northampton and it set the pace for the rest of the season. We won all 18 league games, scoring an average of 48 points a game.

We were truly the best side in the second division and some will say we were in the top four sides in the country. The standards we set that year were of the highest quality and the goals that we wanted to achieve longterm were achieved. We won all our games and gained promotion to Division One; and we made the whole country sit up and take notice of us by the way we played and the standards we set.

These two goals were set out in April 1995 and they were achieved in April 1996, through the whole process of achieving the intermediate and short-term. Each player was set his own goals. They all had to work out for themselves what they wanted to try and achieve, where they wanted to go. The development of the players themselves was as important as the development of the team. The philosophy was: 'If the player knows what he wants, where he is trying to go and how he is going to achieve it, then he will do it and he will understand why he is doing it.' The philosophy ran throughout the year and ensured that the team maintained its high levels of fitness, skill, awareness, and of course success.

## ENGLAND IN SOUTH AFRICA, 1994

South Africa is renowned throughout the world of rugby as one of the hardest places to play. They have a very strong provincial system with many top-class players, perhaps as many as 150 who could play English first division rugby. It is also obviously known as a very volatile country, with areas ranging in attitude and culture, and this was something that would play a huge part in the England tour of 1994.

We went with a large amount of confidence. We'd been together for a long time, we'd had lots of successes and were using this as a springboard for our World Cup campaign the following season.

We had confidence in ourselves, in what we were trying to do and the players that we had there, but were we over confident? South Africa was unknown territory and there is no doubt that we underestimated the strength of the provincial teams.

Our first game was against the Orange Free State, a community keen to demonstrate to South Africans their physical and mental rugby strength. We lost and went on losing. Our overall performances were poor and we struggled to adapt to the game at altitude, on hard grounds and with some fairly inept refereeing. As a team, rather than benefit from these negative aspects, I felt we whinged, moaned and didn't use them positively enough.

However, when the build-up to the First Test began there was a different air about the team. It was obvious from reading the local press that the South Africans had written us off. They made the Springboks out to be clear favourites and this was music to our ears. Despite what we had been doing earlier in the tour, our positive attitude in training and off the field that week was superb and it showed. We scored 24 points in the first sixteen minutes of that first Test at altitude in Pretoria. We played a fast, continuous game, linking backs and forwards on a hard pitch, something that the South Africans believed we couldn't do. We had learnt over the preceding four weeks how to play this type of game. We had learnt what it would require and we went out there and did it. Our inner confidence came through and tactically we were superb on the day.

We then succumbed to what has now become a regular occurrence for an English team. Having beaten one of the world's best sides so convincingly we went out drinking on the Saturday night, and lost all our train of thought, our concentration and our desire. Overnight we went from being determined underdogs to being cocky and self-assured. I was on the bench for the midweek match against Eastern Province and that game will stick with me for the rest of my life. After 19 minutes the England team had lost their captain, Dean Ryan, with a broken hand and their prop with concussion and I was on to take over the captaincy.

The game was as violent as I have ever played in. Heads were being kicked and raked – there was no mercy. It culminated in an incident where the South African second row stood on Jon Callard's head, resulting in him requiring 30 stitches to a head wound. The referee warned the player involved 'not to trample on his head again' and let him off. This infuriated me. I said to the team, 'The next incident we've got to stand our ground.' Unfortunately, the next incident involved me. I was hit twice from the blindside and I reacted. I lost my head, I was out of control and I was fighting. Both Simon Tremaine and I were sent off.

That began some of the toughest few days in my life. I'd been sent off playing for my country. I had let down myself and everyone in the team and in the country. It was a humiliating time for me.

I was allowed to play in the Second Test in Cape Town, but during the build-up I was taken ill and did not eat a meal until the Friday night before the game. Dean Richards was ruled out with an injury, so the England team that had won the First Test a week earlier was disjointed, distracted and at sixes and sevens in terms of motivation to succeed. We were unable to match the mental preparation we had done the week before, though we still believed we could win. As for me, I was worried. I didn't know how far I could go physically and when the game started it was obvious that the opposition were going to try to rile me. What was important for the team was to get ourselves mentally in tune for the task at hand, to try and block out the distractions that occurred mid-week. We were not able to do this.

The only way to do this, in my opinion, is to isolate yourselves and try and iron out the problems together. Talk about what type of distractions there are. Talk about the job in hand and be honest. This is a very personal thing, not easily done, but if the team is a winning team, trusts each other and is well led then the individuals should be forward enough to talk openly about the way they feel. In the long run, this kind of openness will lead to the development of team spirit and trust.

# CHAPTER 3:

# DRIVING ON

Playing sport is an essential part of my life, and playing team sports can be beneficial to an individual in many ways, not just on the sporting front. You may well have trained hard and worked towards your goals within your particular sports, but in team sports it is no good just being an individual. You should have learnt by now that training requires the motivation and the desire to succeed, and usually that involves either a training partner or a training group, and if you are part of a team it can involve other members of your team training with you. Teamwork and the role that you fulfil as an individual in the team is vitally important to the success of that team. Obviously, if an individual in a team is not pulling his weight, not playing well, then the team will fail. Teamwork for me is all about co-operation and respect. In rugby if all fifteen players respect each other and are willing to co-operate with each other, then generally they will all pull in the right direction and you should see winning results. If, however, the team do not respect each other, if they are individuals, self-motivated rather than group motivated, this can lead to failure.

Within the team itself there are always differing characters. There are some people who are louder than others, some who are quieter, but however you are as an individual you have a role to play within the team.

Teamwork doesn't come overnight and a good winning side may take years to develop. The great sides in rugby, for example Bath in the Courage League, have had an outstanding record over the past twelve years. Success like that is not achieved by either buying players in or pushing players beyond their limits. Teamwork comes from each player respecting the others through the long, hard process of training on and off the field, and with that respect comes the desire to play for each other within the side. On top of all of that, if you have a good coach who is tactically leading in the right direction then ultimately the team should not fail.

There is another aspect to teamwork: captaincy. I have been the captain of Northampton Rugby Club for three years. I have in my time led the Club into the second division; I have also led them out of the second division. I have experienced the highs and lows of captaincy. It is not easy. It is often not a job to be envied. Imagine Will Carling – every time he stepped out of the door he had the expectations of the country on his shoulders. Not only did he have the attention of the media and the public, but also he captained a team of fourteen captains, players who in their own right were either captain of their club or senior players within it. It is a master of captaincy who can control and lead fourteen people who think they too could do the job.

At the highest levels the captain takes on many roles. He is obviously responsible for the tactical decisions on the field. He is also responsible for the discipline of the side off the field. He must ensure that his players train hard and maintain standards that he himself sets so that the respect within the team is unerring. He has responsibilities to his players on and off the field. He must be at the front of everything – helping, encouraging, criticising if necessary – but always at the forefront of the team.

Will Carling – probably England's finest captain.

Off the field, at least at the highest level, he is also responsible with the coach for making sure that the players are looked after, that their requests are granted if possible, and their welfare problems (whether financial, personal or rugby-related) taken care of. He may well not be the man who actually does that, but he needs to have one eye looking out for his players at all times to make sure they are well looked after. All of these functions of the captain, if he is to carry them out well, require the ultimate respect from all his players. Without respect the players may become rebellious and not follow him, and not listen to him during key decision-making times under pressure in a game.

One of the best rugby captains I have ever served under was for the Army team. When I first started playing senior rugby, I was picked for the Army to play in the Inter-Services Championship against the Navy and the Air Force. The captain at the time was Brian McCall, big, jovial Irish chap, a major in the Royal Engineers who had represented Ireland five times as a second-row forward. He was without doubt one of the best captains I have ever known, not necessarily because he was the best player or because he was a nice guy, sociable on and off the field, or because he was a disciplinarian. He was able to get the right balance between all aspects of captaincy and he was also able to communicate his needs to the rest of the team without sounding patronising or glib, by being, I guess, human. In the two years that I played with him for the Army XV we won all our games. We did have a good side, but he was a very important part of the team because he was able to motivate all the players, whether young or old, experienced or not. His motivational powers, based on the respect the players had for him, were second to none.

It is not easy for an individual to absorb the pressures involved in being part of a team (and it's even more difficult for the captain). There is pressure within the team and pressure from outside it. Within the team, the pressure due to the expectations of victory or defeat can often lead to tension between the players. This needs to be avoided at all costs, and if the build-up and preparation have been good and the coach and captain lead strongly, then the team should be pulling in the same direction and should emerge with the right solutions; but there will be times when that tension and pressure among the players is evident.

Players also have their own outside pressures, perhaps

family, financial or training. As a captain and as a team member you need to be sympathetic to your team mates' needs and worries and aware of those outside pressures, which can vary depending on the level of sport that you play. If you play international sport then obviously the expectations of the fans and the media can become massive and can lead to a lot of nervous jitters. Learning to cope with such pressures is all part of the individual becoming a world-class player. You shouldn't be afraid to use the hype and expectation to build yourself up, but at the same time calming yourself, controlling yourself, will help you deal with problems that may turn up. A young player thrust into the limelight for the first time, whether with the club or at international level, needs to face those problems and think them through carefully and calmly.

## FEAR OF FAILURE

This is everyone's greatest stumbling block. There is nothing worse than the gut-wrenching trepidation you get in the pit of your stomach before a big fitness session, or if you've been away from training for a few months and you are feeling unfit.

Getting started is very hard. When you start this book with the intention of getting fitter for your sport, there will be a certain amount of fear and trepidation about what you are trying to achieve. Can you do it? This feeling, these energies, can be used in a positive way. If you do feel worried then sit down in a quiet room and analyse the fear itself. Work out why you are afraid. For example, if you are worried about getting started, sit down and weigh it up. Why are doing it? What is your motivation? What are you trying to achieve? At the end of the day your motivation, your reasons for wanting to do something should be greater and should overcome the fear that you feel. Try and use positive thinking as a tool, a past experience where you have had to achieve the goal you didn't think possible. It needn't be with physical fitness, it could even be with business or personal life. Pick out an event that you thought would be unassailable and that you have achieved and use that in a positive way to overcome the fear that you feel. The key to overcoming fear of failure is to analyse it and work out exactly what you are worried about, to weigh it up with the reasons for trying to achieve something. If your reasons and motivation are not great enough you may as well not go on with the book. If you can overcome that initial fear when getting started, you can often find yourself over the biggest hurdle you will meet.

# CHAPTER 4:

# TESTS AND TWEAKS

Now you've got a basic idea of what physical fitness is all about and what Phil and I think the definition of fitness is. Where do you start? Well, as I said before, finding a training partner or someone who knows a bit about training is very helpful, but if you can't find someone then by following our step-by-step guide to fitness training you should be able to achieve it on your own. There is no doubt, however, that having a partner will increase your fitness levels, will help with your motivation and ultimately be better for you.

So where do you start? You have to start with yourself and unfortunately that means tests: not the type you did at school, but fitness tests. There is no other way to do it except to assess yourself. Assess your own body, discover how big you are, what shape you are, how strong you are, how fast you are, how flexible you are and how much fat content you have, and from there you can build up a picture that will help you to develop your first-stage training programme. It sounds horrendous, doesn't it? It's something that until recently I have never enjoyed: I used to hate fitness testing. I hated facing up to the truth and it's something that I tried to avoid at all costs, but you've got to start somewhere and these simple fitness tests will help you discover a bit about yourself, where your strengths and weaknesses lie and the kind of work that you'll need to do to improve.

Lanzarote has been the scene for the England team's fitness testing, which is held annually over the New Year period for a week. You might think that going to Lanzarote, to the sun, sea and sand, is a bit of a holiday, but let me tell you I have been on three training camps and a holiday it most certainly is not. Five days, training twice a day, eating the right food – not a particularly relaxing experience. Recently, now that players work with personal trainers, the emphasis has shifted from fitness testing, as you are required to reach the levels on your own. The time in Lanzarote is now spent building for the Five Nations Championship starting in January. However, the endless hours of testing in Lanzarote left their memories. Doing the bleep test in the gym at 6 a.m. (because that was the coolest time of day) with Dean Richards, Mike Teague, Peter Winterbottom and Martin Bayfield was quite an experience. They taught me one thing and that was to cheat, giving a higher fitness level and keeping Geoff Cooke off your back. Not the attitude of professional sportsmen? Well, back then, that was the way I was: that was how far behind I was in terms of my attitude towards physical fitness and training. Nowadays things are slightly different.

Undoubtedly a major contributor to this fear of fitness testing that I had was the fear of failure. Overcoming that major mental block was something that took a long time, and only through the confidence instilled in me during hard work on the training field, knowing that I could overcome the barriers that were set in front of me, did I become confident ultimately to take fitness tests. These psychological barriers which are thrown up by yourself, ones of fear of failure particularly, are there to be broken down and not turned away from. Once you have overcome these barriers you will enjoy doing fitness tests and enjoy the challenge that you have set yourself.

So what of testing, then? The general idea is to build up a body picture of yourself to discover the areas of weakness you have, so that you can sit down and work out a training programme that is applicable to you, given your sport and your particular weaknesses.

## TEST ONE: AEROBIC ENDURANCE

This is without doubt the worst test of all and one that everybody likes to leave until last. However, my philosophy now, and certainly Phil's, is get it over with first. It's not easy, it's painful, but it has to be done.

There are many types of tests, but the idea is to work out your maximum $VO_2$. The test we use that we think is the best and most relevant is the 12-minute run, or 'Cooper's Test'. There are other methods, such as the bleep test where you carry out repeated 20-metre shuttles to a timed interval, or even the basic 3000-metre-run test, but a 12-minute run is, in our eyes, by far the best.

**Mark out a distance of about 400 metres, whether it is an athletics track – which is preferable – or by simply pacing it out. The idea is to run as many 400 metres as you**

**can in the allotted 12 minutes. Record the distance you covered in the 12 minutes; this is your score.**

It's a killer, but it's simple, easy and can be done anywhere.

## TEST TWO: ANAEROBIC ENDURANCE

You may have thought the last test was bad, but this can be worse. It just depends on your body type. For people who play sports such as rugby, soccer or hockey anaerobic endurance, i.e. running for bursts of activity for between 30 and 90 seconds, it is very relevant. The best and easiest test method is called the repeated sprint test. You will need a partner and a stop watch.

**All you have to do is mark out 40 metres and run flat out over that distance as quickly as you can – timed. You have 20 seconds' rest and you do this 10 times. Therefore you run 10 40-metre sprints with 20 seconds' rest between each – up and down the same track.**

The idea is to take your times and add them together giving you an accumulative score. In six weeks you come back to it and you can measure your times against the test that you did before. You will find, if you are not particularly anaerobically fit, that your times for each 40-metre sprint will get longer and longer as you progress through the test.

## TEST THREE: SPEED

Before you go out and buy yourselves some Linford Christie running pants, just stop. Don't worry about that stuff … yet. This test is simple and easy, and is designed to take a short period of time to complete. Again, you will need a partner with a keen eye and a stop watch.

**There are three distances to be recorded from a standing start: 10 metres, 20 metres and 40 metres. Have two attempts, with at least 2 minutes' rest between trails. Run flat out over the 40-metre course. Note the time at 10, 20 and 40 metres. Record the fastest time. This is your test score.**

## TEST FOUR: STRENGTH

These tests are not designed with champions in mind. There should be no fear of being overwhelmed by them. There are three. We decided to look at two pure strength tests: **one for the chest and arms – the bench press – and one for the legs – the leg press.** In addition there is also a muscular endurance test, which is the **maximum number of press-ups**.

**Note that these tests need to be performed in a gym and you must have an experienced weight trainer to spot for you. Ask any of the instructors in the gym and they will help you.**

### BENCH PRESS

**Practise the bench press movement with a light weight first then guess the maximum weight you think you**

could lift in one movement. With your partner spotting attempt the lift. If the movement was easy, take at least 2 minutes to rest and try again. Try adding 2.5 kg in weight or a weight that you feel is appropriate. If the original weight is too heavy then subtract 2.5 kg. The idea is to achieve your one repetition maximum (1RM) in three or four attempts at most. Eventually you will find your maximum bench press: record the weight.

## LEG PRESS

Warm up with a light weight and get used to the movement. Guess your maximum weight and perform the test as with the bench press. The legs must not bend further

than 90 degrees of knee flexion, i.e. a right angle, before straightening again. Increase the weight until you achieve your one repetition max.

## PRESS-UPS

Perform each movement slowly and accurately and continue this until you are unable to complete another movement. Count your number of press-ups as you are doing it. Record your score.

## TEST FIVE: FLEXIBILITY

We are not looking for Nadia Comaneci, we don't expect anyone to do the splits or put their legs behind their head. Flexibility is, however, a vital part of fitness training. Flexibility tests are notoriously difficult to count because people cheat. We have decided to include two tests and they are focused about the hip and pelvis. A good range of flexibility is important, not only in improving running, but also in preventing injury.

**Note: warm up thoroughly before attempting the stretches. Take the best score of two attempts.**

### STRETCH ONE: SIT AND REACH

**Sit upright and maintain straight legs with your knees locked out, lean forward and reach as far as you can towards or past your toes. Do not allow your knees to bend and do not bounce. Your feet will be pointing straight up and your score is determined by the distance you pass your feet or fall short of your toes when reaching. Get a partner to measure it.**

## STRETCH TWO: BACK EXTENSION

**Lie flat on your front with your arms in a ready position to form a press-up. Arch your back by straightening your arms, try and keep the front of your pelvis, the bony points, as close to the floor as you can. The distance from the bony points to the floor is your score – record it.**

## TEST SIX: BODY COMPOSITION

It is not necessary to test for your body fat composition, providing you exercise regularly and watch what you eat. However, obtaining a skinfold measurement of your body fat composition from your doctor can give you an indication of how 'fat' or how 'thin' you actually are. Remember the old saying 'if you can pinch an inch you're getting fat'.

## TEST SEVEN: SKILL, AGILITY AND BALANCE

The idea here is to put your skill under pressure and see how well you cope. You can make up your own test relevant to your sport, time it and record it. Shown below is a test which was carried out on me by Phil to see how good or bad my ability was to move, turn, pick up and put down a ball under the pressure of time.

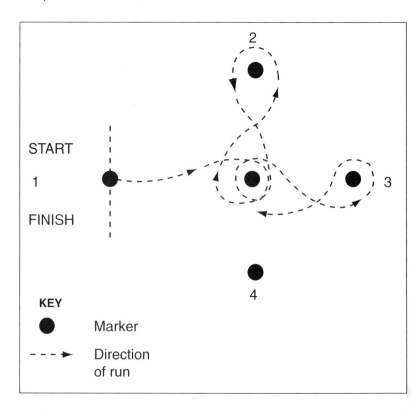

**KEY**

●     Marker

- - - ►     Direction of run

**Start with the ball in hand, run towards the centre and place the ball on the ground, halfway into the square. Run around the centre cone and retrieve the ball, then run around the outside marker number 2 and back towards the centre cone. Again place the ball down midway into the square, run around the centre marker and re-collect the ball. Continue in a similar fashion around markers 3 and 4 and finish by running out of the square by the first marker. Time your attempts and record your score.**

## SELF-ASSESSMENT CHART

| TEST | DATES | | | | |
|---|---|---|---|---|---|
| AEROBIC 12 min run | | | | | |
| ANAEROBIC 10 x 40 m | | | | | |
| SPEED 10 m | | | | | |
| SPEED 20 m | | | | | |
| SPEED 40 m | | | | | |
| STRENGTH Bench press | | | | | |
| STRENGTH Leg Press | | | | | |
| STRENGTH Press-up | | | | | |
| FLEXIBILITY Sit and Reach | | | | | |
| FLEXIBILITY Back Extension | | | | | |
| SKILL | | | | | |

The idea is not to do all the tests in one day. Take a week or so to complete the series of tests, record and date your attempts and then record subsequent attempts every three to six weeks to monitor your progress.

# CHAPTER 5:

# PLANNING THE ROUTE

Most people's idea of a training programme is to train once a week, lunchtime probably because you are so hung over from the night before, and then to play your game on Saturday whether it's squash, rugby, football, tennis or whatever. After the game you suffer all weekend, from the Saturday night until Monday lunchtime, when again you feel guilty and you train. Well, for you out there, those days are over.

Training programmes are there to be followed, not looked at, not talked about, but to be followed; and putting together a training programme is half the battle. Trying to do too much too soon will undoubtedly demoralise you, but a training programme which has been thought through based on your fitness tests, on the type of exercises you want to do for your sport and on your ideas where you think you are weak, can be very beneficial. It is the start of your long road towards a better standard of physical fitness. **Remember, the hardest part is starting ...**

When I was a student, I had a slightly different idea of what a training programme should be. As a student, lectures weren't one of my main priorities – I spent every morning of every day of every week in the gym. For me, to have a body like Arnold Schwarzenegger was what life was all about. I was convinced the girls would come running. Of course, I got stronger, particularly in the arms because that was my favourite exercise, but I never achieved that body and funnily enough the girls barely got past a trot. In those days I had no idea as to how to compile a training programme; putting one together was too far-fetched for me, and of course, drinking every night certainly was not conducive.

When Paul Grayson, the England fly-half, recently took up a heavy-weights training programme he went down to the gym with his and my good friend Martin Hynes. Martin has been pumping heavy weights for many years now as he is a prop forward and needs the extra strength. The two of them set out to find Paul's maximum bench press, as you will be doing. However, they slightly over-estimated Paul's strength and, much to the amusement of the gym staff, when Paul held the bar Martin let go and sure enough, the bar came crashing down on to Paul's chest, partially strangling him. That was just one example of how over-estimating your own strength can wreck a training session. You must plan a good training programme and where to start.

## 1. TIME

The first stage in constructing any training programme is working out how much spare time you've got. It's all well and good for professional athletes who train every day, twice a day, and spend their spare time sleeping and eating. You are probably working, may have families, and have to cope with the constant knocks and injuries which you pick up in sport, so you need to work out your spare time very carefully. In planning your week you need to set aside between one and two hours for training, three times a week. You don't have to train every day, but perhaps on Monday, Wednesday and Friday, or if you compete on a Saturday in team sport then you obviously want Friday off and perhaps you could train Sunday, Monday and Wednesday, obviously it's flexible. You should construct a weekly routine whereby you fill in your playing and training days with your club or sport, and then fill in your own personal sessions to fit around them. Therefore, if you train on a Tuesday and a Thursday night and play on a Saturday, then you need to find three more sessions, perhaps Monday lunchtime, Tuesday lunchtime, and Wednesday lunchtime. This whole process of finding spare time is without doubt the hardest part of constructing a training programme, but once you make the commitment, you need to stick to it. This is particularly relevant early on. Once you get going the programme can be flexible and can fit around other things, but the hardest time is at the very start, so be realistic as to how much time you can spare and you will find it, in the long run, a lot easier.

## 2. AREAS TO WORK

By now you've done all your tests and you should know your strengths and weaknesses. You should produce a list of the areas that you need to work on. If, for example, your aerobic capacity was not particularly good in the tests then you can turn to the aerobic fitness chapter and there you will find a 'revving up' programme that I have done based on building up aerobic fitness. If, on the other hand, it is your strength or speed or anaerobic endurance, then turn to those chapters and you will also find a particular programme based on helping those specific areas.

## 3. IN OR OUT OF SEASON

Obviously, the type of training programme you use will depend on the time of year. If you play a team sport such as rugby or football then you have in- and out-of-season phases. During the in-season period there is a certain type of training that you should do, and the same applies out of season. Shown below are two examples of my training in and out of season: an advanced programme, as I am doing now. You

### OUT OF SEASON

| MONDAY | TUESDAY | WEDNESDAY | THURSDAY | FRIDAY | SATURDAY | SUNDAY |
|---|---|---|---|---|---|---|
| AEROBIC ENDURANCE (long interval) | ANAEROBIC ENDURANCE | | AEROBIC ENDURANCE | | AEROBIC ENDURANCE (cross-training) | R E S T |
| | | SPRINTS | | | | |
| STRENGTH TRAINING | STRENGTH TRAINING | | STRENGTH TRAINING | STRENGTH TRAINING | | |

### IN SEASON

| MONDAY | TUESDAY | WEDNESDAY | THURSDAY | FRIDAY | SATURDAY | SUNDAY |
|---|---|---|---|---|---|---|
| ANAEROBIC TRAINING (interval running) | CLUB TRAINING (including endurance training) | STRENGTH TRAINING Circuit Training | | R E S T | G A M E | LIGHT AEROBIC TRAINING e.g. swim, cycle, jog |
| | | SPRINTS (Speed work) | CLUB TRAINING | | | |
| STRENGTH TRAINING | | | | | | |

will notice there are far more sessions per week during the out-of-season phase. This is because there are no matches and therefore the bumps and bruises and physical exhaustion that you get from playing games is not there. During the season you have to fit in with your club training and your games on a Saturday or whenever you play. Again, this is a very hard area to cope with and to work out, because often you may be suffering still from the Saturday game when you know you have to train hard on a Monday; but no pain, no gain.

## 4. TEAM OR SPORT COMMITMENT

The fourth element to your training programme should be, during the season, the type of commitment you have to give to your chosen sport . For example, if you play rugby, more often than not the club may train on Tuesday and Thursday nights with a game on Saturday, so you need to blank those times out of your weekly programme and adjust your sessions that you may do on a Tuesday and Thursday so that you can still cope with the training in the evening. I have often found that club training can now be very hard and so on a Tuesday and a Thursday I tend not to train during lunchtime. Instead, I have a big session on Monday, two sessions on Wednesday and one on a Sunday.

## 5. FACILITIES

It is advisable to join a good gym. Look around at several – an introductory session is usually free. You will also need to use a track or some kind of open playing fields, even a park. The final ingredient is a simple stopwatch. Nothing flashy, just something you either have on your own watch or a basic hand-held stopwatch. You may find you have to book a gym or a track, and this also plays a part in planning your weekly routine.

## 6. LENGTH OF TRAINING PROGRAMME

Phil and I have always worked on a six-week period as the length of a particular training programme, a micro-cycle. It runs weekly and increases in intensity week after week, so that when you get to the end of the six-week period you should find a marked difference in the areas you are trying to

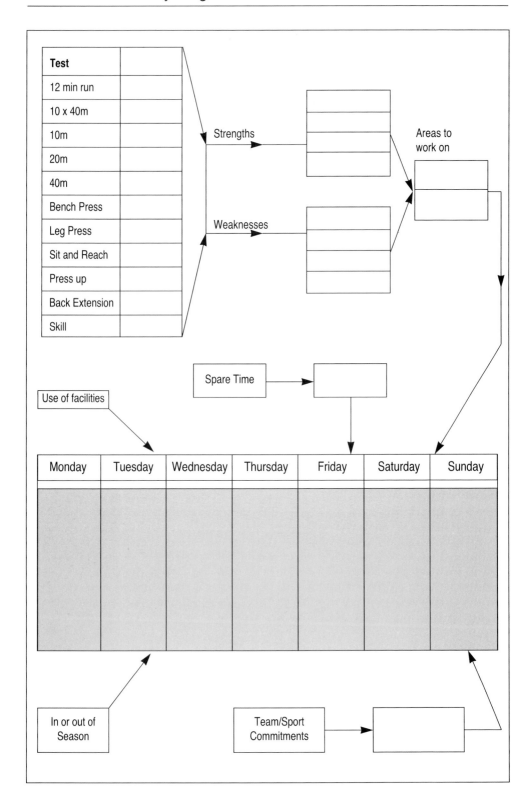

work on. Some people say it should be an eight-week period, and you can do this – it is entirely up to you – but we have found that six weeks is enough. Get some improvement and then you can move on, concentrating on another area and improvement for six more weeks.

The flow chart opposite includes all the different elements that will contribute to your training programme. Start by filling in your test results, working out your areas to work on, and fill in the rest of the blanks. This should give you all the information needed to construct your programme.

# CHAPTER 6:

# REVVING UP

Let's get down to the nitty gritty. This section of the book will outline a *general* step by step **training programme** for you to follow. For convenience the programme is divided into two six-week cycles. Remember, this is a guideline. You may take longer to progress through each six-week micro-cycle. No problem. It may take you a little longer to get there – so what? Responses to training differ with individuals. You may get to a level of fitness you are happy with – if that is the case level off your training there. This level of fitness will then need **maintaining**. To maintain the fitness you have achieved the motor will need **servicing** regularly. At the end of the revving-up period we have outlined a servicing programme that you can set up and follow.

You may well have identified areas of fitness that are a particular weakness to you or that you would like to improve so that you can **fine tune** your fitness. The following chapters on aerobic, anaerobic endurance, speed and strength, all include a **three-week booster programme** that can be used to target these areas.

## GENERAL PROGRAMME FOR THE BEGINNER/ INTERMEDIATE

A possible weekly structure could look like this (day 1 does not have to be a Monday – organise your week to suit yourself):

### 1. OUT OF SEASON

| DAY 1 MONDAY | DAY 2 TUESDAY | DAY 3 WEDNESDAY | DAY 4 THURSDAY | DAY 5 FRIDAY | DAY 6 SATURDAY | DAY 7 SUNDAY |
|---|---|---|---|---|---|---|
| STRENGTH TRAINING | AEROBIC ENDURANCE | STRENGTH TRAINING | ANAEROBIC ENDURANCE | STRENGTH TRAINING | AEROBIC ENDURANCE | |
| WEIGHTS | | WEIGHTS | or | CIRCUIT TRAINING | | R E S T |
| FLEXIBILITY | | | CONTINUOUS RUN | | | |

## WEEK 1

| MONDAY | TUESDAY | WEDNESDAY | THURSDAY | FRIDAY | SATURDAY | SUNDAY |
|---|---|---|---|---|---|---|
| **STRENGTH TRAINING** | **AEROBIC ENDURANCE** | **STRENGTH TRAINING** | **ANAEROBIC ENDURANCE** | **STRENGTH TRAINING** | **AEROBIC ENDURANCE** | R E S T |
| WEIGHTS SPLIT 1* | 2 x 6 min RUNS 3–4 mins REST  70–80% EFFORT | WEIGHTS SPLIT 2 | 3 x 1 min RUNS 90 secs REST or RUN 15 mins  80–90% EFFORT | CIRCUIT TRAINING SPLIT 3 | 2 x 6 min RUNS 3–4 mins REST  70–80% EFFORT | |
| **FLEXIBILITY** | | | | | | |

## WEEK 2

| MONDAY | TUESDAY | WEDNESDAY | THURSDAY | FRIDAY | SATURDAY | SUNDAY |
|---|---|---|---|---|---|---|
| **STRENGTH TRAINING** | **AEROBIC ENDURANCE** | **STRENGTH TRAINING** | **ANAEROBIC ENDURANCE** | **STRENGTH TRAINING** | **AEROBIC ENDURANCE** | R E S T |
| WEIGHTS SPLIT 1 | 3 x 6 min RUNS 3–4 mins REST  70–80% EFFORT | WEIGHTS SPLIT 2 | 4 x 1 min RUNS 90 secs REST or RUN 18 mins  80–90% EFFORT | CIRCUIT TRAINING SPLIT 3 | REPEAT TUESDAY SESSION  70–80% EFFORT | |
| **FLEXIBILITY** | | | | | | |

## WEEK 3

| MONDAY | TUESDAY | WEDNESDAY | THURSDAY | FRIDAY | SATURDAY | SUNDAY |
|---|---|---|---|---|---|---|
| **STRENGTH TRAINING** | **AEROBIC ENDURANCE** | **STRENGTH TRAINING** | **ANAEROBIC ENDURANCE** | **STRENGTH TRAINING** | **AEROBIC ENDURANCE** | R E S T |
| WEIGHTS SPLIT 1 | 1 x 6 min RUN 1 x 5 min RUN 1 x 4 min RUN 2–3 mins REST  70–80% EFFORT | WEIGHTS SPLIT 2 | 5 x 1 min RUNS 90 secs REST or RUN 18 mins  80–90% EFFORT | CIRCUIT TRAINING SPLIT 3 | REPEAT TUESDAY SESSION  70–80% EFFORT | |
| **FLEXIBILITY** | | | | | | |

* See page 98 for explanation of splits.

## WEEK 4

| MONDAY | TUESDAY | WEDNESDAY | THURSDAY | FRIDAY | SATURDAY | SUNDAY |
|---|---|---|---|---|---|---|
| **STRENGTH TRAINING** | **AEROBIC ENDURANCE** | **STRENGTH TRAINING** | **ANAEROBIC ENDURANCE** | **STRENGTH TRAINING** | **AEROBIC ENDURANCE** | **R** |
| WEIGHTS SPLIT 1 | 1 x 6 min RUN 1 x 5 min RUN 2 x 4 min RUNS 2–3 mins REST  70–80% EFFORT | WEIGHTS SPLIT 2 | 2 x 1 min RUNS 90 secs REST 2–3 mins BREAK 4 x 30 sec RUNS 75 secs REST or RUN 21 mins | CIRCUIT TRAINING SPLIT 3 | REPEAT TUESDAY SESSION  70–80% EFFORT | **E S T** |
| **FLEXIBILITY** | | | 80–90% EFFORT | | | |

## WEEK 5

| MONDAY | TUESDAY | WEDNESDAY | THURSDAY | FRIDAY | SATURDAY | SUNDAY |
|---|---|---|---|---|---|---|
| **STRENGTH TRAINING** | **AEROBIC ENDURANCE** | **STRENGTH TRAINING** | **ANAEROBIC ENDURANCE** | **STRENGTH TRAINING** | **AEROBIC ENDURANCE** | **R** |
| WEIGHTS SPLIT 1 | 2 x 5 min RUNS 3 x 4 min RUNS 2–3 mins REST  70–80% EFFORT | WEIGHTS SPLIT 2 | 3 x 1 min RUNS 90 secs REST 2–3 mins BREAK 4 x 30 sec RUNS 75 secs REST or RUN 24 mins | CIRCUIT TRAINING SPLIT 3 | REPEAT TUESDAY SESSION  70–80% EFFORT | **E S T** |
| **FLEXIBILITY** | | | 80–90% EFFORT | | | |

## WEEK 6

| MONDAY | TUESDAY | WEDNESDAY | THURSDAY | FRIDAY | SATURDAY | SUNDAY |
|---|---|---|---|---|---|---|
| **STRENGTH TRAINING** | **AEROBIC ENDURANCE** | **STRENGTH TRAINING** | **ANAEROBIC ENDURANCE** | **STRENGTH TRAINING** | **AEROBIC ENDURANCE** | **R** |
| WEIGHTS SPLIT 1 | 3 x 4 min RUNS 2 x 3 min RUNS 2–3 mins REST  70–80% EFFORT | WEIGHTS SPLIT 2 | 4 x 1 min RUNS 90 secs REST 2–3 mins BREAK 4 x 30 sec RUNS 75 secs REST or RUN 26 mins | CIRCUIT TRAINING SPLIT 3 | REPEAT TUESDAY SESSION  70–80% EFFORT | **E S T** |
| **FLEXIBILITY** | | | 80–90% EFFORT | | | |

## WEEK 7

| MONDAY | TUESDAY | WEDNESDAY | THURSDAY | FRIDAY | SATURDAY | SUNDAY |
|---|---|---|---|---|---|---|
| **STRENGTH TRAINING** | **AEROBIC ENDURANCE** | **STRENGTH TRAINING** | **ANAEROBIC ENDURANCE** | **STRENGTH TRAINING** | **AEROBIC ENDURANCE** | R E S T |
| WEIGHTS SPLIT 1 | 4 x 3 min RUNS 2–3 mins REST 3 x 2 min RUNS 90–120 secs REST | WEIGHTS SPLIT 2 | 'GUT BUSTERS' 3 x 30 sec RUNS 90 secs REST 2–3 mins BREAK 3 x 30 sec RUNS 90 secs REST | CIRCUIT TRAINING SPLIT 3 | REPEAT TUESDAY SESSION 70–80% EFFORT | |
| | 70–80% EFFORT | | 80–90% EFFORT | | | |
| **FLEXIBILITY** | | | | | | |

## WEEK 8

| MONDAY | TUESDAY | WEDNESDAY | THURSDAY | FRIDAY | SATURDAY | SUNDAY |
|---|---|---|---|---|---|---|
| **STRENGTH TRAINING** | **AEROBIC ENDURANCE** | **STRENGTH TRAINING** | **ANAEROBIC ENDURANCE** | **STRENGTH TRAINING** | **AEROBIC ENDURANCE** | R E S T |
| WEIGHTS SPLIT 1 | 3 x 3 min RUNS 2–3 mins REST 4 x 2 min RUNS 90–120 secs REST | WEIGHTS SPLIT 2 | 'GUT BUSTERS' 4 x 30 sec RUNS 90 secs REST 2–3 mins BREAK 3 x 30 sec RUNS 90 secs REST | CIRCUIT TRAINING SPLIT 3 | REPEAT TUESDAY SESSION 70–80% EFFORT | |
| | 70–80% EFFORT | | 80–90% EFFORT | | | |
| **FLEXIBILITY** | | | | | | |

## WEEK 9

| MONDAY | TUESDAY | WEDNESDAY | THURSDAY | FRIDAY | SATURDAY | SUNDAY |
|---|---|---|---|---|---|---|
| **STRENGTH TRAINING** | **AEROBIC ENDURANCE** | **STRENGTH TRAINING** | **ANAEROBIC ENDURANCE** | **STRENGTH TRAINING** | **AEROBIC ENDURANCE** | R E S T |
| WEIGHTS SPLIT 1 | 2 x 3 min RUNS 2–3 mins REST 5 x 2 min RUNS 90–120 secs REST | WEIGHTS SPLIT 2 | 'GUT BUSTERS' 4 x 30 sec RUNS 90 secs REST 3 mins BREAK 4 x 30 sec RUNS 90 secs REST | CIRCUIT TRAINING SPLIT 3 | REPEAT TUESDAY SESSION 80–90% EFFORT | |
| | 80–90% EFFORT | | 90% EFFORT | | | |
| **FLEXIBILITY** | | | | | | |

## WEEK 10

| MONDAY | TUESDAY | WEDNESDAY | THURSDAY | FRIDAY | SATURDAY | SUNDAY |
|---|---|---|---|---|---|---|
| STRENGTH TRAINING | AEROBIC ENDURANCE | STRENGTH TRAINING | ANAEROBIC ENDURANCE | STRENGTH TRAINING | AEROBIC ENDURANCE | R E S T |
| WEIGHTS SPLIT 1 | 6 x 2 min RUNS 90 secs REST 80–90% EFFORT | WEIGHTS SPLIT 2 | 'GUT BUSTERS' 8 x 30 sec RUNS 90 secs REST | CIRCUIT TRAINING SPLIT 3 | REPEAT TUESDAY SESSION 80–90% EFFORT | |
| FLEXIBILITY | | | 90% EFFORT | | | |

## WEEK 11

| MONDAY | TUESDAY | WEDNESDAY | THURSDAY | FRIDAY | SATURDAY | SUNDAY |
|---|---|---|---|---|---|---|
| STRENGTH TRAINING | AEROBIC ENDURANCE | STRENGTH TRAINING | ANAEROBIC ENDURANCE | STRENGTH TRAINING | AEROBIC ENDURANCE | R E S T |
| WEIGHTS SPLIT 1 | 4 x 2 min RUNS 90 secs REST 2–3 mins BREAK 3 x 2 min RUNS 90 secs REST 80–90% EFFORT | WEIGHTS SPLIT 2 | 'GUT BUSTERS' 5 x 30 sec RUNS 90 secs REST 2–3 mins BREAK 4 x 30 sec RUNS 90 secs REST | CIRCUIT TRAINING SPLIT 3 | REPEAT TUESDAY SESSION 80–90% EFFORT | |
| FLEXIBILITY | | | 90% EFFORT | | | |

## WEEK 12

| MONDAY | TUESDAY | WEDNESDAY | THURSDAY | FRIDAY | SATURDAY | SUNDAY |
|---|---|---|---|---|---|---|
| STRENGTH TRAINING | AEROBIC ENDURANCE | STRENGTH TRAINING | ANAEROBIC ENDURANCE | STRENGTH TRAINING | AEROBIC ENDURANCE | R E S T |
| WEIGHTS SPLIT 1 | 4 x 2 min RUNS 90 secs REST 2–3 mins BREAK 4 x 2 min RUNS 90 secs REST 80–90% EFFORT | WEIGHTS SPLIT 2 | 'GUT BUSTERS' 10 x 30 sec RUNS 90 secs REST 90% EFFORT | CIRCUIT TRAINING SPLIT 3 | REPEAT TUESDAY SESSION 80–90% EFFORT | |
| FLEXIBILITY | | | | | | |

## GENERAL PROGRAMME FOR THE ADVANCED SPORTSPERSON

The time commitment is now a little more demanding. The use of back-to-back run/strength sessions may help you organise your time better. A typical week may look like this.

| DAY 1 MONDAY | DAY 2 TUESDAY | DAY 3 WEDNESDAY | DAY 4 THURSDAY | DAY 5 FRIDAY | DAY 6 SATURDAY | DAY 7 SUNDAY |
|---|---|---|---|---|---|---|
| AEROBIC ENDURANCE | SPEED TRAINING | ANAEROBIC ENDURANCE | STRENGTH TRAINING | AEROBIC ENDURANCE | AEROBIC ENDURANCE | R |
| STRENGTH TRAINING | STRENGTH TRAINING | | WEIGHTS SPLIT 3 | | STRENGTH TRAINING | E |
| WEIGHTS SPLIT 1 | CIRCUIT TRAINING SPLIT 2 | | | | WEIGHTS SPLIT 4 | S |
| | | | FLEXIBILITY | | | T |

**'The Firs':** woodland of soft and undulating ground.
**'Sixfields':** this is the name of the running track where we measure and complete these runs.
**'The Hill':** this is our favourite hill – or worst nightmare. A fairly long, drawn-out hill on which we complete these runs.
**'Abi Park':** lovely scenery, murderous changes in slope. Good for the engine.

## WEEK 1    OUT OF SEASON – ADVANCED

| MONDAY | TUESDAY | WEDNESDAY | THURSDAY | FRIDAY | SATURDAY | SUNDAY |
|---|---|---|---|---|---|---|
| AEROBIC ENDURANCE | SPEED TRAINING | ANAEROBIC ENDURANCE | STRENGTH TRAINING | AEROBIC ENDURANCE | AEROBIC ENDURANCE | R |
| 3 x 5 min RUNS 3 mins REST | | 3 x 1 min RUNS 75 secs REST 2 mins BREAK 4 x 30 sec RUNS 75 secs REST | WEIGHTS SPLIT 3 | REPEAT MONDAY SESSION | CROSS-TRAINING MENU | E |
| 70–80% EFFORT | | 90% EFFORT | | | | S |
| STRENGTH TRAINING | STRENGTH TRAINING | 'THE FIRS' | FLEXIBILITY | | STRENGTH TRAINING | T |
| WEIGHTS SPLIT 1 | CIRCUIT TRAINING SPLIT 2 | | | | WEIGHTS SPLIT 4 | |

See page 107 for explanation of splits.

## WEEK 2

| MONDAY | TUESDAY | WEDNESDAY | THURSDAY | FRIDAY | SATURDAY | SUNDAY |
|---|---|---|---|---|---|---|
| **AEROBIC ENDURANCE** | **SPEED TRAINING** | **ANAEROBIC ENDURANCE** | **STRENGTH TRAINING** | **AEROBIC ENDURANCE** | **AEROBIC ENDURANCE** | R E S T |
| 4 x 4 min RUNS 2–3 mins REST<br><br>70–80% EFFORT | | 4 x 1 min RUNS 75 secs REST 2 mins BREAK 5 x 30 sec RUNS 75 secs REST<br><br>90% EFFORT | WEIGHTS SPLIT 3 | REPEAT MONDAY SESSION | CROSS-TRAINING MENU | |
| **STRENGTH TRAINING** | **STRENGTH TRAINING** | 'THE FIRS' | **FLEXIBILITY** | | **STRENGTH TRAINING** | |
| WEIGHTS SPLIT 1 | CIRCUIT TRAINING SPLIT 2 | | | | WEIGHTS SPLIT 4 | |

## WEEK 3

| MONDAY | TUESDAY | WEDNESDAY | THURSDAY | FRIDAY | SATURDAY | SUNDAY |
|---|---|---|---|---|---|---|
| **AEROBIC ENDURANCE** | **SPEED TRAINING** | **ANAEROBIC ENDURANCE** | **STRENGTH TRAINING** | **AEROBIC ENDURANCE** | **AEROBIC ENDURANCE** | R E S T |
| 3 x 4 min RUNS 2 mins REST 2 mins BREAK 2 x 3 min RUNS 2 mins REST<br><br>70–80% EFFORT | | 4 x 1 min RUNS 60 secs REST 2 mins BREAK 6 x 30 sec RUNS 75 secs REST<br><br>90% EFFORT | WEIGHTS SPLIT 3 | REPEAT MONDAY SESSION | CROSS - TRAINING MENU | |
| **STRENGTH TRAINING** | **STRENGTH TRAINING** | 'THE FIRS' | **FLEXIBILITY** | | **STRENGTH TRAINING** | |
| WEIGHTS SPLIT 1 | CIRCUIT TRAINING SPLIT 2 | | | | WEIGHTS SPLIT 4 | |

## WEEK 4

| MONDAY | TUESDAY | WEDNESDAY | THURSDAY | FRIDAY | SATURDAY | SUNDAY |
|---|---|---|---|---|---|---|
| **AEROBIC ENDURANCE** | **SPEED TRAINING** | **ANAEROBIC ENDURANCE** | **STRENGTH TRAINING** | **AEROBIC ENDURANCE** | **AEROBIC ENDURANCE** | R E S T |
| 5 x 3 min RUNS 2 mins REST<br><br>70–80% EFFORT | | 4 x 1 min RUNS 1 min REST 2 mins BREAK 8 x 30 sec RUNS 75 secs REST<br><br>90% EFFORT | WEIGHTS SPLIT 3 | REPEAT MONDAY SESSION | CROSS-TRAINING MENU | |
| **STRENGTH TRAINING** | **STRENGTH TRAINING** | 'THE FIRS' | **FLEXIBILITY** | | **STRENGTH TRAINING** | |
| WEIGHTS SPLIT 1 | CIRCUIT TRAINING SPLIT 2 | | | | WEIGHTS SPLIT 4 | |

## WEEK 5

| MONDAY | TUESDAY | WEDNESDAY | THURSDAY | FRIDAY | SATURDAY | SUNDAY |
|---|---|---|---|---|---|---|
| **AEROBIC ENDURANCE** | **SPEED TRAINING** | **ANAEROBIC ENDURANCE** | **STRENGTH TRAINING** | **AEROBIC ENDURANCE** | **AEROBIC ENDURANCE** | R E S T |
| 2 x 3 min RUNS 2 mins REST 2 mins BREAK 4 x 2 min RUNS 2 mins REST<br><br>70–80% EFFORT | | 4 x 1 min RUNS 75 secs REST 2 mins BREAK 8 x 30 sec RUNS 1 min REST<br><br>90% EFFORT<br><br>'THE FIRS' | WEIGHTS SPLIT 3 | REPEAT MONDAY SESSION | CROSS-TRAINING MENU | |
| **STRENGTH TRAINING** | **STRENGTH TRAINING** | | **FLEXIBILITY** | | **STRENGTH TRAINING** | |
| WEIGHTS SPLIT 1 | CIRCUIT TRAINING SPLIT 2 | | | | WEIGHTS SPLIT 4 | |

## WEEK 6

| MONDAY | TUESDAY | WEDNESDAY | THURSDAY | FRIDAY | SATURDAY | SUNDAY |
|---|---|---|---|---|---|---|
| **AEROBIC ENDURANCE** | **SPEED TRAINING** | **ANAEROBIC ENDURANCE** | **STRENGTH TRAINING** | **AEROBIC ENDURANCE** | **AEROBIC ENDURANCE** | R |
| 2 x 3 min RUNS 2 mins REST 2 mins BREAK 5 x 2 min RUNS 2 mins REST | | 4 x 1 min RUNS 75 secs REST 2 mins BREAK 8 x 30 sec RUNS 1 min REST | WEIGHTS SPLIT 3 | REPEAT MONDAY SESSION | CROSS-TRAINING MENU | E S T |
| 70–80% EFFORT | | 90% EFFORT 'THE FIRS' | | | | |
| **STRENGTH TRAINING** | **STRENGTH TRAINING** | | **FLEXIBILITY** | | **STRENGTH TRAINING** | |
| WEIGHTS SPLIT 1 | CIRCUIT TRAINING SPLIT 2 | | | | WEIGHTS SPLIT 4 | |

## WEEK 7

| MONDAY | TUESDAY | WEDNESDAY | THURSDAY | FRIDAY | SATURDAY | SUNDAY |
|---|---|---|---|---|---|---|
| **AEROBIC ENDURANCE** | **SPEED TRAINING** | **ANAEROBIC ENDURANCE** | **STRENGTH TRAINING** | **AEROBIC ENDURANCE** | **AEROBIC ENDURANCE** | R |
| 8 x 2 min RUNS 75 secs REST | | 4 x 300m RUNS 90 secs REST 2 mins BREAK 4 x 200m RUNS 90 secs REST | WEIGHTS SPLIT 3 | REPEAT MONDAY SESSION | CROSS-TRAINING MENU | E S T |
| 80–90% EFFORT | | | | | | |
| **STRENGTH TRAINING** | **STRENGTH TRAINING** | 90% EFFORT | **FLEXIBILITY** | | **STRENGTH TRAINING** | |
| WEIGHTS SPLIT 1 | CIRCUIT TRAINING SPLIT 2 | 'SIXFIELDS' | | | WEIGHTS SPLIT 4 | |

## WEEK 8

| MONDAY | TUESDAY | WEDNESDAY | THURSDAY | FRIDAY | SATURDAY | SUNDAY |
|---|---|---|---|---|---|---|
| **AEROBIC ENDURANCE** | **SPEED TRAINING** | **ANAEROBIC ENDURANCE** | **STRENGTH TRAINING** | **AEROBIC ENDURANCE** | **AEROBIC ENDURANCE** | R |
| 9 x 2 min RUNS 75 secs REST<br><br>80–90% EFFORT | | 4 x 300m RUNS 4 x 200m RUNS 2 x 150m RUNS ALL 90 secs REST 2–3 mins BREAK<br><br>90% EFFORT | WEIGHTS SPLIT 3 | REPEAT MONDAY SESSION | CROSS-TRAINING MENU | E S T |
| **STRENGTH TRAINING** | **STRENGTH TRAINING** | 'SIXFIELDS' | **FLEXIBILITY** | | **STRENGTH TRAINING** | |
| WEIGHTS SPLIT 1 | CIRCUIT TRAINING SPLIT 2 | | | | WEIGHTS SPLIT 4 | |

## WEEK 9

| MONDAY | TUESDAY | WEDNESDAY | THURSDAY | FRIDAY | SATURDAY | SUNDAY |
|---|---|---|---|---|---|---|
| **AEROBIC ENDURANCE** | **SPEED TRAINING** | **ANAEROBIC ENDURANCE** | **STRENGTH TRAINING** | **AEROBIC ENDURANCE** | **AEROBIC ENDURANCE** | R |
| 10 x 2 min RUNS 75 secs REST<br><br>80–90% EFFORT | | 4 x 300m RUNS 4 x 200m RUNS 2 x 150m RUNS ALL 90 secs REST 2–3 mins BREAK<br><br>90% EFFORT | WEIGHTS SPLIT 3 | REPEAT MONDAY SESSION | CROSS-TRAINING MENU | E S T |
| **STRENGTH TRAINING** | **STRENGTH TRAINING** | 'SIXFIELDS' | **FLEXIBILITY** | | **STRENGTH TRAINING** | |
| WEIGHTS SPLIT 1 | CIRCUIT TRAINING SPLIT 2 | | | | WEIGHTS SPLIT 4 | |

## WEEK 10

| MONDAY | TUESDAY | WEDNESDAY | THURSDAY | FRIDAY | SATURDAY | SUNDAY |
|---|---|---|---|---|---|---|
| **AEROBIC ENDURANCE** | **SPEED TRAINING** | **ANAEROBIC ENDURANCE** | **STRENGTH TRAINING** | **AEROBIC ENDURANCE** | **AEROBIC ENDURANCE** | R E S T |
| 4 x 2 min RUNS 75 secs REST 2 mins BREAK 4 x 1 min RUNS 75 secs REST 80–90% EFFORT | | 4 x 25 sec RUNS 75–90 secs REST 2–3 mins BREAK 4 x 25 sec RUNS 75–90 secs REST | WEIGHTS SPLIT 3 | REPEAT MONDAY SESSION | CROSS-TRAINING MENU | |
| **STRENGTH TRAINING** | **STRENGTH TRAINING** | 90–100% EFFORT | **FLEXIBILITY** | | **STRENGTH TRAINING** | |
| WEIGHTS SPLIT 1 | CIRCUIT TRAINING SPLIT 2 | 'THE HILL' | | | WEIGHTS SPLIT 4 | |

## WEEK 11

| MONDAY | TUESDAY | WEDNESDAY | THURSDAY | FRIDAY | SATURDAY | SUNDAY |
|---|---|---|---|---|---|---|
| **AEROBIC ENDURANCE** | **SPEED TRAINING** | **ANAEROBIC ENDURANCE** | **STRENGTH TRAINING** | **AEROBIC ENDURANCE** | **AEROBIC ENDURANCE** | R E S T |
| 4 x 2 min RUNS 75 secs REST 2 min BREAK 5 x 1 min RUNS 75 secs REST 80–90% EFFORT | | 5 x 25 sec RUNS 75–90 secs REST 2–3 mins BREAK 5 x 25 sec RUNS 75–90 secs REST | WEIGHTS SPLIT 3 | REPEAT MONDAY SESSION | CROSS-TRAINING MENU | |
| **STRENGTH TRAINING** | **STRENGTH TRAINING** | 90–100% EFFORT | **FLEXIBILITY** | | **STRENGTH TRAINING** | |
| WEIGHTS SPLIT 1 | CIRCUIT TRAINING SPLIT 2 | 'THE HILL' | | | WEIGHTS SPLIT 4 | |

**WEEK 12**

| MONDAY | TUESDAY | WEDNESDAY | THURSDAY | FRIDAY | SATURDAY | SUNDAY |
|---|---|---|---|---|---|---|
| **AEROBIC ENDURANCE** | **SPEED TRAINING** | **ANAEROBIC ENDURANCE** | **STRENGTH TRAINING** | **AEROBIC ENDURANCE** | **AEROBIC ENDURANCE** | R E S T |
| 4 x 2 min RUNS 75 secs REST 2 mins BREAK 6 x 1 min RUNS 75 secs REST<br><br>80–90% EFFORT | | 10 x 25 sec RUNS 75–90 secs REST<br><br>90–100% EFFORT<br><br>'THE HILL' | WEIGHTS SPLIT 3 | REPEAT MONDAY SESSION | CROSS-TRAINING MENU | |
| **STRENGTH TRAINING** | **STRENGTH TRAINING** | | **FLEXIBILITY** | | **STRENGTH TRAINING** | |
| WEIGHTS SPLIT 1 | CIRCUIT TRAINING SPLIT 2 | | | | WEIGHTS SPLIT 4 | |

## 2. IN SEASON

Once you have achieved that level of fitness how do you hold on to it? Like a car engine, your body needs regular servicing – keep the training going. We feel that it is probably true that you are at your fittest the moment you start the first game of the season. It's all downhill from then as games, injury and time all get in the way of training!! Always remember though, you are **training to play the game – not for training's sake.**

A maintenance or **servicing programme** that will help keep or even improve fitness levels during the season is pretty easy to construct. We have designed a service programme for the beginner/intermediate and advanced sportsperson. We have left a space for you to design your own. For each training session choose one of the programmes outlined in the **revving-up** section or the **strength training** or **speed training** chapters. In essence build your own from our training schedule and use sessions from the week 7–12 programme in each section.

## MAINTENANCE PROGRAMME FOR THE BEGINNER/INTERMEDIATE

| MONDAY | TUESDAY | WEDNESDAY | THURSDAY | FRIDAY | SATURDAY | SUNDAY |
|---|---|---|---|---|---|---|
| **ANAEROBIC ENDURANCE** | **CLUB TRAINING** | **SPEED TRAINING** | **CLUB TRAINING** | R | G | **FLEXIBILITY** |
| | | and/or | | E | A | |
| | | | | S | M | |
| **STRENGTH TRAINING** | | **STRENGTH TRAINING** | | T | E | **EASY AEROBIC EXERCISE** |
| WEIGHTS or CIRCUIT TRAINING | | WEIGHTS or CIRCUIT TRAINING | | | | e.g. swim, cycle, run |

Compile your own:

| DAY 1 | DAY 2 | DAY 3 | DAY 4 | DAY 5 | DAY 6 | DAY 7 |
|---|---|---|---|---|---|---|
| | | | | | | |

## MAINTENANCE PROGRAMME FOR THE ADVANCED

| MONDAY | TUESDAY | WEDNESDAY | THURSDAY | FRIDAY | SATURDAY | SUNDAY |
|---|---|---|---|---|---|---|
| **ANAEROBIC ENDURANCE** | **CLUB TRAINING** | **SPEED TRAINING** | **CLUB TRAINING** | R | G | **FLEXIBILITY** |
| | (HARD) | and/or | (EASY) | E | A | |
| | | | | S | M | |
| **STRENGTH TRAINING** | | **STRENGTH TRAINING** | | T | E | **EASY AEROBIC EXERCISE** |
| WEIGHTS | | CIRCUIT TRAINING | | | | e.g. swim, cycle, run |
| | | | | **FLEXIBILITY** | | |

### Compile your own:

| DAY 1 | DAY 2 | DAY 3 | DAY 4 | DAY 5 | DAY 6 | DAY 7 |
|---|---|---|---|---|---|---|
| | | | | | | |
| | | | | | | |
| | | | | | | |

# CHAPTER 7

# ENDURANCE –

## LE MANS

Before you turn the page and get quickly on to another chapter just stop. No matter where you go and no matter what you do, you cannot get away from this type of exercise. Aerobic endurance, or the ability to run at a lower intensity of your maximum work rate but for a longer duration, is the key to success in virtually every sport. Sports like rugby, hockey and soccer rely on a high level of aerobic endurance. Without this base, the speed, strength and power that can come later on in training cannot be developed to its maximum. Although this is without doubt the worst area for me and many bigger framed men, it is an essential area and one that I have worked on so hard over the past three years that I now feel confident in my aerobic endurance.

So what is aerobic endurance exactly? Well, as I said, it's an exercise which relies on your ability to take in oxygen for a long period of time at a steady rate so that the muscles can keep on working. When you see the marathon runners coming in to the last three or four miles unsteady on their feet, this is from fuel depletion in the muscles. You generally find in any type of long-distance running, marathon canoeing, long-distance cycling, swimming, etc., that the people who take up this kind of sport have a very high aerobic endurance. All of their training is designed to increase it. This lovely phrase 'max $VO_2$' indicates as we explained earlier the body's capacity to consume oxygen at a maximum rate. This is what max $VO_2$ is short for. Having a high max $VO_2$ means that you have a greater aerobic endurance. Or, in simple terms, you can carry on running for longer than someone who's got a low max $VO_2$. Large $VO_2$s are not the be-all and end-all. They do not mean you are instantly good at your sport, because many sports also demand physical and mental strength as well as technical skill, but there is no doubt that having a high max $VO_2$ gives you an excellent starting point on which you can start progressive training for your sport.

The test we gave you to determine your aerobic fitness will

ot give you a figure for your max VO$_2$. It is not necessarily mportant, what you need to concentrate on is the distance hat you have travelled during that 12-minute run. Obviously, ou are trying to increase that distance as a measure of how nuch fitter you are becoming.

So what type of exercise do you need to carry out to mprove your aerobic endurance? This is where we get to the nard stuff. As I have said before, your aerobic endurance is he base on which you can build all your other types of raining, your strength, your speed and your power, but that comes later. First your aerobic base. Pre-season is the most mportant time for this training, before you enter competitions. 3ecause of the debilitating factor of these types of aerobic exercises, it is not advisable to do them during the season when there are games on. That is why during pre-season you end to find a lot of aerobic work being done.

*(Opposite page) Noureddine Morceli, built for the test of long-distance running with large, powerful legs, smaller upper body.*

## TYPES OF EXERCISES

You do not have to go out and do a 5-mile run to increase your aerobic endurance; you do not have to go out and do a wo-hour cycle ride. If you run for five minutes at a high ntensity and then a short rest and then run again for five ninutes, you're working your aerobic system predominantly. _ess than that, for example two minutes, is a mixture of your aerobic and your anaerobic system. For many team sport players, it is best that you work around the aerobic/anaerobic hreshold, i.e. the point at which energy production is primarily aerobic. This can be achieved by training using hree-minute runs and two-minute runs. Over the past three years Phil and I have found that the three-minute and two-minute run base will give you a very good aerobic training. Programmes below are based on three-minute runs at 70 to 30 per cent of maximum effort and two-minute runs at 80 to 90 per cent of maximum, with approximately ninety seconds o rest between each run. As the weeks go by during your raining programme, you can increase the number of repeats. This type of running is without doubt the hardest you will ever do. For me, the big person, it is particularly gut-wrenching. It's all right for the whippets who tend to fly around at a steady rate and carry no weight, but as I said to Phil, 'Try running with a sack of spuds on your back, mate, and then you'll now what it's really all about.'

As you can see, there are training programmes in Chapter Six which Phil and I carried out in and out of season, that are called 'revving-up programmes'. If you wanted to blast the aerobic system in or out of season, that is the sort o programme you can use as a guide when you are starting your programmes. The other beginner and advanced weekly programmes demonstrate the type of running that you wil have to do during weeks 1–6 and weeks 7–12 in order to increase your aerobic endurance. This exercise should be enough, but if you are starting from scratch give yoursel more time, don't expect to be Sebastian Coe overnight – i won't happen. What you must do is work hard, keep to the times, keep to the rest times, so that you can monitor yoursel daily, and sure enough, if you do the exercises that are written down and you work hard you will succeed in getting yourself aerobically fitter. At the end of the day there are no other excuses, no way out. These types of exercises require hard work and graft.

Aerobic sessions do not all need to be about running There are three other types of aerobic session that we use swimming, rowing and cycling. These can be thrown in purely to break up the monotony. If, for example, you're struggling with an injury to one of your legs, then obviously swimming is a good option, using a leg float. If you are struggling with an injury to your shoulder then cycling is a good option. All three types of exercise work your aerobic system, and opposite again, you can see the types of progression and types o exercises which you need to carry out when you cycle, swim and row to increase your aerobic capacity. As you know, the swimming, cycling and running combination forms one of the most gruelling sports in the world – that of triathlon. It's one o Phil's loves – God knows why – a competition where, in the long distance version, he had to swim 2½ miles, cycle 120 miles and run a full marathon. Now, correct me if I'm wrong but you have got to be slightly demented to want to do that but Phil did it and he finished in the top 400. It shows wha can be achieved through just hard graft and dedication. A combination of all three disciplines – running, swimming cycling – gives you a really good work-out, but if you are a rugby player, a footballer, or a hockey player, then doing continuous endurance work is not conducive to the type o body structure you want. As a rugby player, you need aerobic endurance – 'runability', muscle strength, power and speed As a footballer you need endurance with speed and powe and as a hockey player again you need endurance with speed and power and of course a certain amount of strength. Getting the balance right is all-important. Of course, if you are following this programme and you are an Ironman triathlete then crack on, you lunatic!!

The sessions outlined below are suitable for all trainers. I would expect the advanced sportsperson to perform the activity a little harder, faster, and with a greater level of intensity throughout. Set target times and try and beat them throughout the 6–12-week period. Remember, **variety is the spice of life**. Training should not become boring and monotonous.

## CROSS-TRAINING

Mix and match your own session from weeks 4–7.

### PROGRESSIONS

| WEEK | 1 | 2 | 3 | 4 | 5 | 6 | 7–12 |
|---|---|---|---|---|---|---|---|
| CYCLE<br><br>TARGET | 30 mins<br>80–90%<br>10 miles | 40 mins<br>80–90%<br>13 miles | 50 mins<br>80–90%<br>16 miles | 60 mins<br>80–90%<br>20 miles | INCREASE TIME OR DISTANCE COVERED | | |
| Swim | 400m | 600m | 800m | 2 x 400m<br>3 mins break | 2 x 400m<br>2 mins break | 2 x 500m<br>3 mins break | 1 x 1000m |
| Row | 3 x 1000m | 2 x 2000m | 2 x 2000m<br>+<br>1 x 500m | 2 x 2500m | 1 x 5000m | 1 x 5000m | |
| or | | 4 x 1000m | | 2 x 2000m<br>+<br>1 x1600m | 2 x 2500m | | |

## 'FINE TUNING' AEROBIC FITNESS: BEGINNER/INTERMEDIATE

### THREE-WEEK IN-SEASON BOOSTER PROGRAMME

#### WEEK 1

| MONDAY | TUESDAY | WEDNESDAY | THURSDAY | FRIDAY | SATURDAY | SUNDAY |
|---|---|---|---|---|---|---|
| **AEROBIC ENDURANCE** | | **AEROBIC ENDURANCE** | | R E S T | G A M E | **AEROBIC ENDURANCE** |
| 4 x 3 min RUNS 90 secs REST 80% EFFORT | **CLUB TRAINING** | 6 x 2 min RUNS 90 secs REST 90% EFFORT | **CLUB TRAINING** | | | CROSS- TRAINING MENU |
| **STRENGTH TRAINING** | | **FLEXIBILITY** | | | | |
| CIRCUIT TRAINING | | | | | | |

#### WEEK 2

| MONDAY | TUESDAY | WEDNESDAY | THURSDAY | FRIDAY | SATURDAY | SUNDAY |
|---|---|---|---|---|---|---|
| **AEROBIC ENDURANCE** | | **AEROBIC ENDURANCE** | | R E S T | G A M E | **AEROBIC ENDURANCE** |
| 5 x 3 min RUNS 2 mins REST 80% EFFORT | **CLUB TRAINING** | 8 x 2 min RUNS 90 secs REST 90% EFFORT | **CLUB TRAINING** | | | CROSS- TRAINING MENU |
| **STRENGTH TRAINING** | | **FLEXIBILITY** | | | | |
| CIRCUIT TRAINING | | | | | | |

#### WEEK 3

| MONDAY | TUESDAY | WEDNESDAY | THURSDAY | FRIDAY | SATURDAY | SUNDAY |
|---|---|---|---|---|---|---|
| **AEROBIC ENDURANCE** | | **AEROBIC ENDURANCE** | | R E S T | G A M E | **AEROBIC ENDURANCE** |
| 3 x 3 min RUNS 2 mins REST 4 x 2 min RUNS 90 secs REST 80–90% EFFORT | **CLUB TRAINING** | 3 x 3 min RUNS 2 mins REST 6 x 3 min RUNS 90 secs REST 90% EFFORT | **CLUB TRAINING** | | | CROSS- TRAINING MENU |
| **STRENGTH TRAINING** | | **FLEXIBILITY** | | | | |
| CIRCUIT TRAINING | | | | | | |

## 'FINE TUNING' AEROBIC FITNESS: ADVANCED

### THREE-WEEK IN-SEASON BOOSTER PROGRAMME

### WEEK 1

| MONDAY | TUESDAY | WEDNESDAY | THURSDAY | FRIDAY | SATURDAY | SUNDAY |
|---|---|---|---|---|---|---|
| AEROBIC ENDURANCE | SPEED TRAINING | AEROBIC ENDURANCE | | R E S T | G A M E | AEROBIC ENDURANCE |
| 5 x 3 min RUNS 2 mins REST 80% EFFORT | CLUB TRAINING | 8 x 2 min RUNS 90 secs REST 90% EFFORT | CLUB TRAINING | | | CROSS-TRAINING MENU |
| STRENGTH TRAINING | | FLEXIBILITY | | FLEXIBILITY | | FLEXIBILITY |
| CIRCUIT TRAINING | | | | | | |

### WEEK 2

| MONDAY | TUESDAY | WEDNESDAY | THURSDAY | FRIDAY | SATURDAY | SUNDAY |
|---|---|---|---|---|---|---|
| AEROBIC ENDURANCE | SPEED TRAINING | AEROBIC ENDURANCE | | R E S T | G A M E | AEROBIC ENDURANCE |
| 6 x 3 min RUNS 2 mins REST 80% EFFORT | CLUB TRAINING | 10 x 2 min RUNS 90 secs REST 90% EFFORT | CLUB TRAINING | | | CROSS-TRAINING MENU |
| STRENGTH TRAINING | | FLEXIBILITY | | FLEXIBILITY | | FLEXIBILITY |
| CIRCUIT TRAINING | | | | | | |

### WEEK 3

| MONDAY | TUESDAY | WEDNESDAY | THURSDAY | FRIDAY | SATURDAY | SUNDAY |
|---|---|---|---|---|---|---|
| AEROBIC ENDURANCE | SPEED TRAINING | AEROBIC ENDURANCE | | R E S T | G A M E | AEROBIC ENDURANCE |
| 3 x 3 min RUNS 2 mins REST 6 x 2 min RUNS 75 secs REST 90% EFFORT | CLUB TRAINING | 3 x 3 min RUNS 2 mins REST 8 x 2 min RUNS 75 secs REST 90% EFFORT | CLUB TRAINING | | | CROSS-TRAINING MENU |
| STRENGTH TRAINING | | FLEXIBILITY | | FLEXIBILITY | | FLEXIBILITY |
| CIRCUIT TRAINING | | | | | | |

## SPORTS PROFILES

Marathon runners and similar long-duration, low-intensity athletes work the aerobic system throughout. A very specific type of muscle fibre is usually predominant in this type of athlete: slow-twitch muscle fibre. Because of the nature of the sport such runners and swimmers tend to be lightweight with a very low fat percentage, but with considerably strong legs in the case of the long-distance runner. The reason for the low fat is that they tend to metabolise fat during such long events and convert it into glycogen. In the marathon runner's case, the monitoring of his diet, the nutrition and his rest during training is very important. Obviously, you cannot train for marathon running by running marathons, but most marathon runners tend to run miles and miles every week to condition themselves for such a long-distance, long-duration event. They are, however, prone to over-training and therefore are associated with a lot of injuries. The classic marathon runner's injuries are a non-specific knee pain or shin splints, which are both brought on by running miles in shoes that are worn out or inappropriate for that type of sport.

Sprinters and explosive throwers are a very different type of athlete, exactly the opposite to a marathon runner in terms of the type of muscle they are trying to develop. Predominantly, fast-twitch muscle fibre is evident in sprinters and throwers. In their training, they develop explosive, powerful bursts of energy which are relevant to their event. This type of explosive system uses the ATP-CP system (Adenozine triphosphate-creotin phosphate). This system only works for a maximum of about ten seconds and is an all-out, non-oxygen-requiring system, which tends to lead to quick fatigue. Most of the work done by these athletes takes place in the gym. They work on developing strength with speed for powerful movements. They work not only on the legs, but also on the upper body. It is a closed skill and has a specific set of movements. Success is built on speed and strength, which equals power. Such types of athletes tend to get traumatic types of injury which are associated with quick and forceful muscle contractions – hamstring pulls or shoulder strains, for instance.

Tennis players develop a general fitness for all parts of the body. Specifically, however, they need to concentrate on aerobic work, as often a five-set match in the heat of Flushing

Liz McColgan –
Britain's finest
distance runner.

Linford Christie:
speed plus
strength equals
power.

Meadow, New York, for example, requires a high level o
endurance, both mental and physical. The concentratior
factor that tennis players have to contend with is
phenomenal. During a match they do however need shor
bursts of anaerobic activity, such as occur during a shorte
rally. They are only running small distances in a court, but a
high intensity, therefore they tend to work on their shor
speed endurance as well as their aerobic endurance.

Steffi Graf: not just a tennis player, but a superb all-round athlete.

Upper body strength for a tennis player is important because hitting the ball, particularly in a service, is a powerful movement. The stronger the individual generally, the more powerfully he or she can hit the ball. So a tennis player will work his upper body in the gym. However, the exercises tend to be based more around muscular endurance rather than strength, because strength training may increase the size of the muscles a little too much. Unlike rugby players, tennis players can train by playing tennis. The specificity of training principle is easy to apply in this case. Tennis players' injuries tend to be associated with repetitive strain, i.e. a repetitive stretch or contraction of muscle under a good deal of force can lead to problems such as tennis elbow or achilles tendinitis.

Most footballers and hockey players train by playing their own sport, and the principles are the same for both. They are both based on high aerobic level, because both are continuous running games. They also require short sprinting ability, therefore short bursts of anaerobic activity, so as well as doing their longer-duration, low-intensity aerobic work, they will work on sprint training – high intensity, short duration. They also need to have the explosive strength and power that is used in either kicking the ball in football or hitting it in hockey. Both are

Perhaps Britain's most talented footballer: Ryan Giggs.

contact sports, although not to the same degree as rugby, and so a general type of upper body work-out is usually needed.

Footballers tend to be all legs and no upper body. This is due to their specific type of training – running, five-a-side soccer and so on. Hockey players are often bigger; they need to have the strength in the shoulders and the arms for hitting the ball. Injuries to both usually occur as a result of external forces, that is to say opponents in contact situations. Soccer players predominantly sustain lower-limb injuries in tackling such as knee ligament strains. Hockey players are at risk from flying balls.

*Sean Kerly ready to strike. Dedication to training led Great Britain's hockey team to Olympic Gold in the 1988 Olympics.*

And now for Allan Lamb's unique views on fitness – rather surprising for such an undoubtedly great player!

Fitness has never been a top priority for most cricketers – I do not think cricketers are fitness freaks like rugby, football and tennis players. During the early stages of my career, I never worked too much on my fitness, but as I grew older I felt it was more necessary. I enjoyed running but I had awful problems with my calves and hamstrings.

Whilst touring the West Indies in 1990 we had a great deal

of very physical work in Barbados in the early part of the tour. One afternoon Goochie, who is a fitness freak, decided to run back from the cricket ground to the hotel, which was about seven or eight miles. Robin Smith and myself decided to join him, under protest of our physio Laurie Brown who advised us not to run as we already had a very vigorous work out ('for a cricketer'). So off we went at a brisk pace through Bridgetown which is about two miles from the cricket ground and six miles from the hotel. I decided to increase the pace but within five minutes of doing so, I felt a very sharp pain in my right calf. It felt like someone had shot me in the leg. Goochie and Judge showed no signs of sympathy and said they would see me back at the hotel – if I was not there by the time they got there, they would come and fetch me.

Well, it was not easy getting a car to stop, never mind a taxi! Eventually a car pulled up and the Barbadian said, 'Hey, Lamby, where are you going?' Thank goodness I was a cricketer as he recognised me.

I replied, 'The Rocky Resort Hotel.'

'Hop in and I'll take you.'

Well, I was the laughing stock on arrival at the hotel as all my team mates greeted me. The moral of the story is – I always carry a 'cab card' on me!!

Goochie, as I said earlier, is a real fitness freak. He would go for a run at 6 a.m., come back, use the weights and then go to cricket training. He believes that fitness has helped his game and certainly he has a record to prove it. He is forty-two and still playing first-class cricket with success.

Now Botham and Gower, on the other hand, definitely do not fall into the category of fitness freaks. Botham never did any physical training as he believed he got fit bowling a game (but not nets because he never bowled there), and running between the wickets, which he did not do very often as he hit boundaries all the time. Gower was no fitness champion: running between wickets and fielding got him fit, plus the odd bottle of Bollinger to keep up his stamina!!

Cricket has become more aware of fitness these days and most clubs keep a record of their players' fitness and their diet.

My fitness training consisted of the following routine by the time I ended my career:

- A couple of miles of road running – if I did not break down.

Allan Lamb in full flow.

- Different stretching exercises, which were very important for me, especially for my calves and hamstrings.
- Light weights at the gym for my shoulders, forearms and legs.

Diets never played a big part while I was playing. I slowed down on the lager and beer, but always had a drink or two before and during a Test Match which relieved me when trying to fend off those fast bowlers! Overall, there were no restrictions on what we drank or ate.

The game was there to be enjoyed!

# CHAPTER 8

# ENDURANCE –
## SHORT BURSTS

Now you've got yourself up with a good aerobic base, the rest of the training and, certainly for me and Phil, the more enjoyable parts of training can begin. Building up that base ensures you are going to be able to work on specific areas of your fitness: your strength, your speed which will come later, and now your anaerobic endurance. This anaerobic endurance is particularly relevant to sports in which you, the player, may repeat high-intensity activities followed by a short rest again and again and again. In a game of football, for example, the player needs to be sprinting or moving quickly at one moment, then a short rest and he's doing it again. This type of activity when you're working at a high intensity of your maximum, perhaps 80–90% and beyond, with short periods of rest, is called anaerobic endurance.

What exactly happens to the body during anaerobic exercise? Well, if you remember, during aerobic exercise, oxygen is used to produce energy within your muscles, and at a low intensity the system of producing energy can function quite happily. However, in circumstances where you are working at a higher intensity using energy at a fast rate, it is impossible for your body and the aerobic system to produce enough. Anaerobic metabolism produces the extra energy required.

The repeated sprint test is designed so that for the last few sprints you should be approaching fatigue: if you are not, then you are not working hard enough to stress the anaerobic energy system.

To increase your anaerobic endurance the type of exercises you need are short bursts, usually between 15 and 60 seconds of running at around 80 to 90 or 95 per cent effort. As you have already seen, there is a programme that I have done for the fine tuning period to increase my anaerobic endurance. You will see that most of the running is based around the one-minute interval, but at a very high intensity workrate. You will also see an in-season and an

## ATP AND LACTIC ACID

So what really is energy, how do we get it, where does it come from? Quite simply, energy in the muscle is ATP and for those of you who are science buffs, that stands for adenozine triphosphate (a dosing what?). ATP is an energy-rich compound that acts as an immediate source for most energy-requiring processes in the body, particularly, and most relevant to us, in the action of muscle contraction. ATP molecules are broken down within the body and one of the derivatives of this reaction is free energy. It is this energy which is used in the contraction of muscle fibres. Stores of ATP within the muscles are limited and are replaced to avoid fatigue. This process occurs in two ways: in the presence of oxygen *aerobically* or without the presence of oxygen *anaerobically*. ATP is replaced by the aerobic or anaerobic metabolism of stored fuels such as carbohydrates and fats. So where does lactic acid come in? Well, in this process of anaerobic metabolism where ATP is produced without the process of oxygen, high-intensity exercise can only last for between 60 and 90 seconds. A by-product of this reaction is lactic acid. Lactic acid built up in large enough amounts is associated with fatigue and results in a ceasing of physical activity.

out-of-season training programme on a progressive weekly basis for both intermediate, beginner and advanced. Again, the same principles apply as in the aerobic chapter. This kind of fitness does not occur overnight and you cannot expect to achieve higher results without the aerobic base described in the previous chapter.

In the season and in normal maintenance training programmes, a combination of both aerobic and anaerobic running is good and will help you maintain your aerobic and anaerobic fitness, but obviously if you need to boost or fine tune your anaerobic endurance you need to pursue the type of programme that follows. You will notice some of the sessions have names. This is not an attempt to humanise our programmes because at the end of the day they are just times and distances, but the names became synonymous with places or the fear and trepidation that Phil and I felt before attempting some of these runs. They are not easy. Some people think that the anaerobic type of training is harder than the aerobic. Personally, I prefer the anaerobic type of work. Phil, I think, prefers the aerobic type of work. As you will already know the difference between the two is very small, but certainly when you do your anaerobic training you will realise that you do have to work at a very much higher percentage of running than when you are doing aerobic training. This can result in a pretty sick feeling. Martin Bayfield, the England second row, is renowned for this sick feeling. In Bedford where he trains he uses a park where there is a particularly conveniently placed hill. He uses this hill for his one-minute runs, which start on a nice flat path and finish with 50 metres up a very steep hill. He has been known to frighten people walking their dogs by being sick at the top of this hill. On one occasion he was verbally abused by a very upset old lady.

One of the best sessions we do is the hill session. This is a hill covering a distance of about 150 metres, on which we do up to ten hill sprints with one minute's rest. Ian Hunter, who is an excellent trainer, went up this hill alone one day and came back into the gym very flustered and obviously a bit shocked. It transpired that on the eighth repetition, when he was starting to feel tired, a large dog emerged from behind the bushes and proceeded to chase him up the hill. He wasn't too perturbed about this because he thought he could outrun it. What disturbed him slightly was when the owner emerged after the dog shouting, 'Keep running, keep running.' Ian stepped on the gas and must have run about 300 metres before he came to a wall which he vaulted and escaped the attentions of the dog.

## 'FINE TUNING' ANAEROBIC FITNESS: BEGINNER/INTERMEDIATE

### THREE-WEEK IN-SEASON BOOSTER PROGRAMME

**WEEK 1**

| MONDAY | TUESDAY | WEDNESDAY | THURSDAY | FRIDAY | SATURDAY | SUNDAY |
|---|---|---|---|---|---|---|
| **ANAEROBIC TRAINING** 'GUT BUSTER' 4 x 30 sec RUNS 90 secs REST 2–3 mins BREAK REPEAT 90% EFFORT | **CLUB TRAINING** | **ANAEROBIC TRAINING** 4 x 20 sec RUNS 90 secs REST 2–3 mins BREAK REPEAT 90% EFFORT 'THE HILL' | **CLUB TRAINING** | R E S T **FLEXIBILITY** | G A M E | **EASY AEROBIC ENDURANCE** CROSS-TRAINING MENU |

**WEEK 2**

| MONDAY | TUESDAY | WEDNESDAY | THURSDAY | FRIDAY | SATURDAY | SUNDAY |
|---|---|---|---|---|---|---|
| **ANAEROBIC TRAINING** 'GUT BUSTER' 5 x 30 sec RUNS 90 secs REST 2–3 mins BREAK REPEAT 90% EFFORT | **CLUB TRAINING** | **ANAEROBIC TRAINING** 5 x 20 sec RUNS 90 secs REST 2–3 mins BREAK REPEAT 90% EFFORT 'THE HILL' | **CLUB TRAINING** | R E S T **FLEXIBILITY** | G A M E | **EASY AEROBIC ENDURANCE** CROSS-TRAINING MENU |

**WEEK 3**

| MONDAY | TUESDAY | WEDNESDAY | THURSDAY | FRIDAY | SATURDAY | SUNDAY |
|---|---|---|---|---|---|---|
| **ANAEROBIC TRAINING** 2 x 1 min RUNS 90 secs REST 3 x 30 sec RUNS 90 secs REST 4 x 40m SPRINTS 20 secs REST 90% EFFORT 'ABI PARK' | **CLUB TRAINING** | **ANAEROBIC TRAINING** 3 x 1 min RUNS 90 secs REST 3 x 30 sec RUNS 90 secs REST 4 x 40m SPRINTS 20 secs REST 2 mins BREAK 4 x 40m SPRINTS 20 secs REST 90% EFFORT 'ABI PARK' | **CLUB TRAINING** | R E S T **FLEXIBILITY** | G A M E | **EASY AEROBIC ENDURANCE** CROSS-TRAINING MENU |

## 'FINE TUNING' ANAEROBIC FITNESS: ADVANCED

### THREE-WEEK IN-SEASON BOOSTER PROGRAMME

#### WEEK 1

| MONDAY | TUESDAY | WEDNESDAY | THURSDAY | FRIDAY | SATURDAY | SUNDAY |
|---|---|---|---|---|---|---|
| ANAEROBIC ENDURANCE | STRENGTH TRAINING | ANAEROBIC ENDURANCE | | R E S T | G A M E | EASY AEROBIC ENDURANCE |
| 4 x 25 sec RUNS 75 secs REST 2–3 mins BREAK 3 x 25 sec RUNS 75 secs REST 90% EFFORT 'THE HILL' | WEIGHTS SPLIT 4 | 3 x 1 min RUNS 90 secs REST 2 mins BREAK 3 x 30 sec RUNS 75 secs REST 2 mins BREAK 6 x 40m RUNS 20 secs REST 90% EFFORT | CLUB TRAINING | | | CROSS-TRAINING MENU |
| STRENGTH TRAINING | CLUB TRAINING | 'ABI PARK' | | FLEXIBILITY | | |
| WEIGHTS SPLIT 3* | | | | | | |

#### WEEK 2

| MONDAY | TUESDAY | WEDNESDAY | THURSDAY | FRIDAY | SATURDAY | SUNDAY |
|---|---|---|---|---|---|---|
| ANAEROBIC ENDURANCE | STRENGTH TRAINING | ANAEROBIC ENDURANCE | | R E S T | G A M E | EASY AEROBIC ENDURANCE |
| 4 x 25 sec RUNS 75 secs REST 2–3 mins BREAK REPEAT 'THE HILL' 90% EFFORT | WEIGHTS SPLIT 4 | 4 x 1 min RUNS 90 secs REST 2 mins BREAK 4 x 30 sec RUNS 75 secs REST 2 mins BREAK 4 x 40m RUNS 20 secs REST 2 mins BREAK 4 x 40m RUNS | CLUB TRAINING | | | CROSS-TRAINING MENU |
| STRENGTH TRAINING | CLUB TRAINING | 90% EFFORT | | FLEXIBILITY | | |
| WEIGHTS SPLIT 3 | | 'ABI PARK' | | | | |

* See page 107 for explanation of splits.

## 'FINE TUNING' ANAEROBIC FITNESS: ADVANCED

### THREE-WEEK IN-SEASON BOOSTER PROGRAMME

**WEEK 3**

| MONDAY | TUESDAY | WEDNESDAY | THURSDAY | FRIDAY | SATURDAY | SUNDAY |
|---|---|---|---|---|---|---|
| **ANAEROBIC ENDURANCE** | **STRENGTH TRAINING** | **ANAEROBIC ENDURANCE** | | R E S T | G A M E | **EASY AEROBIC ENDURANCE** |
| 5 x 25 sec RUNS 75 secs REST 2–3 mins BREAK | WEIGHTS SPLIT 4 | 4 x 1 min RUNS 90 secs REST 2 mins BREAK 5 x 30 sec RUNS 75 secs REST 2 mins BREAK 4 x 40m RUNS 20 secs REST 2 mins BREAK 5 x 40m RUNS 20 secs REST | **CLUB TRAINING** | | | CROSS-TRAINING MENU |
| REPEAT 'THE HILL' | **CLUB TRAINING** | | | | | |
| **STRENGTH TRAINING** | | 90% EFFORT | | **FLEXIBILITY** | | |
| WEIGHTS SPLIT 3 | | 'ABI PARK' | | | | |

# CHAPTER 9

# STRENGTH

Strength is important in sport as it helps in performing skilled activities such as running, jumping, pumping iron or catching. Secondly it is sports-specific – a prop in rugby needs to be strong enough to scrummage and 'rip ball'. A scrum-half has to be strong enough to 'break tackles' or 'hand off' opponents. A judo player always needs incredible strength. Thirdly, strength of muscles is important in protecting joints and preventing injury. *Three* good reasons for strength training.

## WHAT IS STRENGTH?

**Pure Strength** is often described as the greatest force (or torque) that a muscle or group of muscles can produce in a single maximum effort. A person who can lift a heavier weight than another person in a certain way can be said to be stronger. Is this very useful in sports? Maybe in some sports such as athletics or weight lifting, but not so much in team games such as soccer and rugby. If, however, that second sportsperson can lift a heavier weight 15 repetitions more than the first he is said to have greater **muscle endurance**. This might be more appropriate in many sports. **Power** is the 'buzz word' in rugby these days. This is somewhere between pure strength and muscle endurance and relates to the speed with which muscle strength can be used to generate force. It stands to reason that power requires strength, speed and some muscle endurance from the performer. To cope with all the demands of rugby we use weight training and circuit training to develop pure strength, muscle endurance and power. It is worth bearing in mind that leg strength can be developed by activities such as anaerobic running and sprinting as well.

**REMEMBER: building up strength at the expense of muscle endurance or running ability is not the way forward in developing a better sports player. An all-round**

**and well-balanced approach to training *is* the way forward.**

Not one for the model agency.

> There was a young man named Tim Rodber who turned up at Northampton Rugby Club with bodybuilder's (Popeye) arms, but no chest or leg development. A clear case of macho weight training, and an unbalanced training routine. Looked good in short-sleeved shirts – not so useful on the rugby pitch.

## EFFECTS OF STRENGTH TRAINING

There is an ancient story of Milo of Cretona who was said to carry a full-grown bull over his head around the Olympic arenas of the sixth century BC. He apparently achieved this by lifting the bull above his head each day from when it was a calf until it was fully grown. As the bull got heavier he got stronger. This is a clear example of the main principle of weight training – namely that **progressive resistive exercise** will increase strength. By progressively overloading specific muscles with heavier resistance or weights near to or at maximum level those muscles will adapt and get stronger.

Unfortunately, or perhaps fortunately, your capacity for muscle strength is largely determined by physiological factors, such as the size and type of your muscle fibre, as well as the anatomical lever advantages offered by your bone and muscle structure. Is this why props are so strong? They are big-muscled, but short and stocky, with short levers – they fatigue quickly.

## PHYSICAL DIFFERENCES

If you are an older female sportsperson with slightly built muscle, which is all slow-twitch fibre, then you are pretty disadvantaged in the strength stakes. Muscle fibre type and size, gender and age are all important in determining your strength and possibly strength potential.

Each sportsperson will have slow-twitch or fast-twitch muscle fibre in different proportions within his or her muscle. Slow-twitch muscle is more adapted to longer-duration sub-maximal activity and is pretty fatigue resistant but not so good at producing pure strength or power.

Fast-twitch muscle is more adapted to short-duration maximal activity and fatigues quickly. It is very good at producing strength and power movements.

In sports such as rugby it is an advantage to have a greater proportion of fast-twitch muscle which will allow the development of strength and power.

Females who weight-train are extremely unlikely to become muscle bound, although they will get stronger. Males have a greater ability to gain strength and bulk with weight training due to the presence of male sex hormones. It has been shown that strength gains in males sharply increase with training at puberty and decline from the age of 30 when testosterone levels begin to decline. Unless your girlfriend is taking male hormone tablets, she is unlikely to develop into a female equivalent of the Incredible Hulk. There is no good reason for sportswomen to stay away from the weights.

Greater strength gains through training are found in larger muscles: this is another unfair advantage of sportsmen over sportswomen, as males at nearly every age have a larger muscle cross-sectional area than females and therefore respond to training more readily.

Better strength gains, through weight training, are found between the ages of puberty and the early to mid-30s. That is not to say that younger and older sportspeople cannot benefit from strength training. Beware of training with heavy weights before puberty though, as bones are not fully mature and may be damaged. This is not proven, but not worth taking the risk. Strength and power can be developed by lighter work-outs and of course **circuit training** using bodyweight exercises.

## TRAINING PRINCIPLES

It is worth noting that strength is speed, angle and range of movement specific for any activity. We feel that dynamic exercises rather than static are more skill-related and we use progressive resistant exercise as our regime for improving strength. So that you can decide which weight to begin with for each exercise, and to test if progress is being made, use the one repetition maximum principle (1RM).

1RM = the biggest weight that can be lifted at one time with correct form or action for a predetermined exercise.

To discover what your 1RM is, first guesstimate the weight. If the exercise is completed too easily, add an appropriate weight – one, two or five kilos. If it is too difficult reduce the weight by similar amounts. The 1RM should be found within three or four attempts.

---

### OLD WIVES' TALES

**Weight trainers become muscle bound:** this is not true. Most lifters demonstrate good, if not above average, joint flexibility.

**Muscle turns to fat:** this is not physiologically possible. You may get weaker and smaller muscles if you stop training. If you continue to eat vast amounts and stop training you may get fatter. Muscle fibre, though, does not turn into fat at any time.

## TRAINING PROGRAMMES

### 'REVVING UP' OUT OF SEASON: BEGINNER/ INTERMEDIATE

A quick look at Chapter Six showing the general programme reveals three weight-training slots per week. The programme below has been split into three parts and should be followed in order. (Splits 1 and 2 are weight training exercises and Split 3 is circuit training.)

**Weeks 1–6**     Work out your 1RM for each exercise. For this period perform: 3 sets of 12–15 repetitions with about 50% of 1RM for each exercise.

**Weeks 7–I2**     Reassess your 1RM for each exercise, then work as follows: 3 sets of 8–10 repetitions with about 60–80% of 1RM.

**Note: you should be struggling to complete the last repetition of each set.**

## WEIGHT TRAINING

| SPLIT (1) | SPLIT (2) |
|---|---|
| Bold entries mean that these exercises can be Supersetted. That is, perform a set of each exercise alternately until the workout is complete. This restricts the amount of 'waiting around'. | |
| **CHEST/BACK/ABDOMINALS** | **SHOULDERS/ARMS/LEGS** |
| 1. **Bench Press** | 1. Half Squat |
| 2. **Pull-Ups/chins** | 2. **Shoulder Press** |
| 3. Crunches* | 3. **Bicep Curls** |
| 4. **Inclined Bench Press** | 4. Hamstring Curls |
| 5. **Lateral Pull-downs** | 5. **Lateral Raises** |
| 6. Crossover Crunches* | 6. **Tricep Pull-downs** |
| 7. **Inclined Dumbell Press** | 7. Quads Extension |
| 8. **Upright Rowing** | 8. **Seated Dumbell Press** |
| 9. Sit-ups* | 9. **Narrow-handed Bench Press** |

* Abdominal exercises can be performed depending on your own ability.

## CIRCUIT TRAINING

### SPLIT (3)

| | |
|---|---|
| 1. Press-Ups | 6. Dips (between two chairs) |
| 2. Crunches | 7. Crossover Crunches |
| 3. Squat Jumps | 8. Star Jumps |
| 4. Backlifts | 9. Narrow-handed Press-ups |
| 5. Squat Thrusts | 10. High-knee Sprinting |

Pull-Ups/chins

Press-Ups

## Crunches

## Squat Jumps

Backlifts

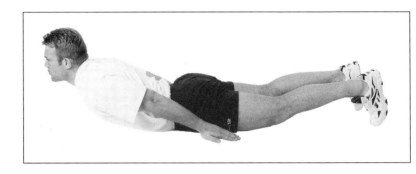

Squat Thrusts

Dips

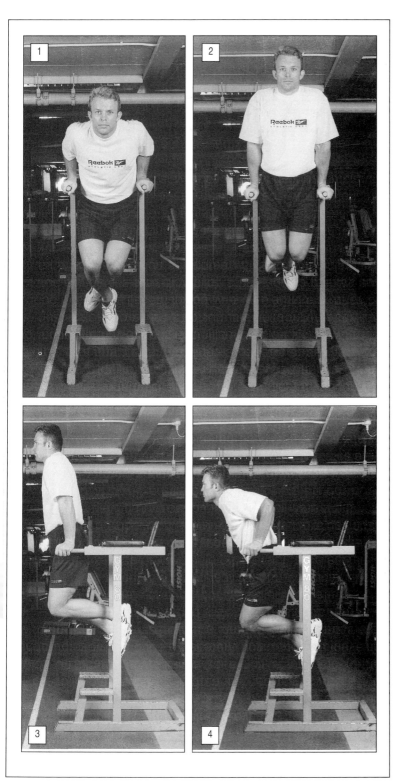

Crossover Crunches

Star Jumps

Narrow-handed
Press-ups

High-knee Sprinting

Burpees

Step Ups

1    2    3

## Circuit Training:

**How It Works:** work out how many repetitions you can achieve for each exercise in one minute. Divide this number by two to give you your **work rate (WR)**.

**Do this circuit:**

**Weeks 1–6**    Three-sets of 1 x WR with 20 seconds' rest between each exercise.

**Weeks 7–12**    Three to four sets of 1 x WR with no rest between each exercise.

## REVVING UP OUT OF SEASON: ADVANCED STRENGTH TRAINING

Again, a quick look at the general programme in Chapter Six

shows provision for four strength-training sessions made up of weight training and a possible circuit training.

The programme below has been split into four parts – splits 1, 3 and 4 are weight training, and split 2 is circuit training.

**Weeks 1–6**    Work out your 1RM for each exercise. For this period perform 3–4 sets at 8–10 repetitions with about 60–80% of 1RM for each exercise.

**Weeks 7–12**    Reassess your 1RM for each exercise, then perform 3 sets of 12–15 repetitions with about 50–70% of 1RM.

**Note: you should be struggling to perform the last repetition of each set.**

**Circuit Training:**

**How it works**: perform the exercises in sequences. No rest is allowed between exercises. At the end of each circuit take 30–60 seconds recovery period. **Perform exercises correctly with good form.**

**Do these circuits:**

**Weeks 1–6**    Three circuits. Build up number of repetitions for each exercise. **Time yourself.**

**Weeks 7–12**    Four circuits. **Set and beat target times** as you progress.

**SERVICING IN-SEASON STRENGTH TRAINING**

This section is relevant for both beginner/intermediate and advanced trainers. A quick look at the training programmes in Chapter Six for servicing or maintenance during the season shows that two strength-training sessions are included during the week.

**Beginners/Intermediate:** the two sessions should either be:

1. Both circuit training, or
2. One weight training and one circuit training.

## WEIGHT TRAINING

| SPLIT (1) | SPLIT (3) | SPLIT (4) |
|---|---|---|
| Bold entries mean Superset. One set of each of these exercises is performed alternately to save time and increase work rate during the sessions. | | |
| LEGS/ABDOMINALS | SHOULDERS/ARMS | CHEST/BACK |
| 1. Half Squats | 1. Shoulder Press | 1. Flat Bench Press |
| 2. Crunches* | 2. Bicep Curls | 2. Seated Rowing |
| 3. Hamstring Curls | 3. Lateral Raises | 3. Incline Bench Press |
| 4. Crossover Crunches* | 4. Tricep Extension | 4. Upright Row |
| 5. Quadriceps Extensions | 5. Seated Dumbell Press | 5. Incline Flyes |
| 6. Reverse Crunches* | 6. Narrow-handed Bench Press | 6. Chins |
| 7. Calf Raises | | 7. Dips* |
| 8. Leg Raises | | |

\* These exercises can be performed with repetition numbers dependent on your own ability.

## CIRCUIT TRAINING
## SPLIT (2)

| EXERCISE | REPETITIONS | EXERCISE | REPETITIONS |
|---|---|---|---|
| 1. Step-ups | 15–20 each leg | 9. Back/Shoulder Lifts | 8–10 |
| 2. Press-ups | 15–20 | 10. Squat Thrusts | 15–20 |
| 3. Squat Jumps | 10–14 | 11. Dips (between chairs) | 15–20 |
| 4. Sit-ups/Crunches | 15–20 | 12. Narrow-handed Press-ups | 8–12 |
| 5. Burpees | 10–14 | 13. (Pull-ups – if equipment available) | 6–10 |
| 6. Crossover Sit-ups/Crunches | 15–20 | 14. Shuttle Run 10m course | 20 seconds |
| 7. Clap Press-ups | 6–10 | | |
| 8. High Knees (running on the spot) | 20 each leg | | |

This should help maintain most of the strength, power and muscle endurance gained during the 'revving-up' period.

**Advanced:** the first session during the week is usually a heavier weight-training session. The midweek session is always circuit training. Choose from the strength-training sessions outlined in the 'revving-up' section from weeks 7–12.

**Note: if you are feeling 'heavy legged' during games then back off the leg exercises.**

### FINE TUNING STRENGTH-TRAINING BOOSTER PROGRAMME

It is virtually impossible to boost strength during the season because of injuries, knocks and lack of time. Certainly a three-week intense programme is likely to have little effect – so you will be looking at a six-week concentrated effort. Everything about strength training is for longterm benefits, not short-term gains. Some physiologists these days are talking about five-year training programmes.

A booster programme for both beginners/intermediate and advanced trainers may involve organising the training week as highlighted below.

| BEGINNER/INTERMEDIATE | | | | | | |
|---|---|---|---|---|---|---|
| MONDAY | TUESDAY | WEDNESDAY | THURSDAY | FRIDAY | SATURDAY | SUNDAY |
| STRENGTH TRAINING | | STRENGTH TRAINING | STRENGTH TRAINING | R E S T | G A M E | R E S T |
| WEIGHTS SPLIT 1 | CLUB TRAINING | WEIGHTS SPLIT 2 | CIRCUIT TRAINING SPLIT 3 | | | |
| ANAEROBIC TRAINING | | SPEED TRAINING | CLUB TRAINING | | | |
| | | SPRINTS | | | | |

| ADVANCED | | | | | |
|---|---|---|---|---|---|
| MONDAY | WEDNESDAY | THURSDAY | FRIDAY | SATURDAY | SUNDAY |
| STRENGTH TRAINING | STRENGTH TRAINING | STRENGTH TRAINING | R E S T | G A M E | EASY AEROBIC EXERCISE |
| WEIGHTS SPLIT 1 | WEIGHTS SPLIT 2 | CIRCUIT TRAINING SPLIT 3 | | | e.g. swim, cycle, run |
| ANAEROBIC TRAINING | SPEED TRAINING | CLUB TRAINING | | | |
| | SPRINTS | | | | |

## Key points:

- You are unlikely to notice strength gains with less than three training sessions per week. One or two training sessions per week will help maintain your level of strength.

- Make sure your technique is sound – ask for advice.

- Allow 48 hours between strength-training sessions on the same muscle groups (if using a 'split' regime, training can be on consecutive days).

- Wear a belt if possible to support lower back.

- Rest and adequate diet are as important as training.

- If you already have your own strength routine, stick with it.

## Technique:

- Warm up, cool down and stretch at each session.

- Perform each contraction slowly and under control.

- Aim for steady improvement.

# CHAPTER 10:

# SPEED

Some people are faster than others and that's often the result of inheriting more *fast-twitch* muscle fibres than *slow-twitch*. Speed is a direct function of how fast you can move your legs – cadence – and the length of your stride. As important in sport is the ability to *accelerate* and to show a *change of pace* – that is, shift gear.

You may be at a biological disadvantage, blame your parents – but *all* of us can actually get faster by improving what we already possess. *Speed* can be improved by developing running technique and improving sprinting power. We try to achieve this by practising certain running drills as part of a specific sprints-training session. We always end our quality sprints session with pressure – back-to-back – sprints! Just for fun!

In addition to speed-training sessions, your strength and anaerobic training will enhance your power and ability to sprint.

Speed training demands quality, and after a good warm-up and stretch the drills should be performed precisely, with control and power. Allow good recovery. The sprinting pressure drill comes at the end

It is difficult to progress a speed session as it is really quality not quantity we are after here – so you will notice very little difference between sessions.

A typical speed session will look like:

| | |
|---|---|
| Warm-up: | 6–12 mins jogging |
| Stretching: | 5–10 mins |
| Drill: | legs only |
| | arms and legs |
| Bounding Activities (plyometrics) | |
| Running Drills: | acceleration, change in pace etc. |
| Pressure Sprints | |
| Warm-down/Stretch | |

As this is a *quality* session the same practices and progressions can be followed by the beginner/intermediate or advanced sportsperson. Plenty of rest and plenty of power are the only prerequisites. Blast yourself silly at the end.

### SPEED TRAINING: REVVING UP
### BEGINNER/INTERMEDIATE AND ADVANCED

| WEEK 1 | WEEK 2 | WEEK 3 | WEEK 4 |
|---|---|---|---|
| WARM UP/STRETCH | WARM UP/STRETCH | WARM UP/STRETCH | WARM UP/STRETCH |
| DRILLS: | DRILLS: | DRILLS: | DRILLS: |
| KNEES 3 x 15m<br>FLICKS 3 x 15m | 4 x 15m<br>4 x 15m | 4 x 20m<br>4 x 20m | 4 x 25m<br>4 x 25m |
| BOUNDING: | BOUNDING: | BOUNDING: | BOUNDING: |
| DOUBLE LEG 4 x 10m | 4 x 15m | 4 x 20m | 4 x 20m |
| SKILL: | SKILL: | SKILL: | SKILL: |
| DRIVES 4 x 30m | 5 x 30m | 5 x 30m | 6 x 30m |
| SPRINTS: | SPRINTS: | SPRINTS: | SPRINTS: |
| 4 x 30m<br>30 secs REST | 4 x 30m<br>20 secs REST | 4 x 30m<br>30 secs REST | 4 x 30m<br>30 secs REST |

| WEEK 5 | WEEK 6 | WEEK 7 | WEEK 8 |
|---|---|---|---|
| WARM UP/STRETCH | WARM UP/STRETCH | WARM UP/STRETCH | WARM UP/STRETCH |
| DRILLS: | DRILLS: | DRILLS: | DRILLS: |
| KNEES 4 x 20m<br>FLICKS 4 x 20m<br>SPEED 4 x 20m | 4 x 20m<br>4 x 20m<br>4 x 20m | 4 x 20m<br>4 x 20m<br>4 x 20m | 4 x 20m<br>4 x 20m<br>4 x 20m |
| BOUNDING: | BOUNDING: | BOUNDING: | BOUNDING: |
| SPEED HOPS 3 x 15m | 4 x 15m | 4 x 20m | 4 x 25m |
| SKILL: | SKILL: | SKILL: | SKILL: |
| INS AND OUTS x 3 | x 4 | x 4 | x 5 |
| SPRINTS | SPRINTS | SPRINTS | SPRINTS |
| 2 x 4 x 30m<br>30 secs REST<br>2–3 mins BREAK | 2 x 4 x 30m<br>4 x 30m<br>20 secs REST<br>2–3 mins BREAK | 2 x 4 x 30m<br>20 secs REST<br>2–3 mins BREAK | 3 x 4 x 30m<br>20 secs REST<br>2–3 mins BREAK |

## SPEED TRAINING: REVVING UP     INTERMEDIATE AND ADVANCED

| WEEK 9 | WEEK 10 | WEEK 11 | WEEK 12 |
|---|---|---|---|
| WARM UP/STRETCH | WARM UP/STRETCH | WARM UP/STRETCH | WARM UP/STRETCH |
| DRILLS: | DRILLS: | DRILLS: | DRILLS: |
| AS WEEKS 5–8 | AS WEEKS 5–8 | AS WEEKS 5–8 | AS WEEKS 5–8 |
| BOUNDING: | BOUNDING: | BOUNDING: | BOUNDING: |
| JUMP SPRINT x 4 | x 5 | x 6 | x 8m |
| SKILL: | SKILL: | SKILL: | SKILL: |
| GEAR CHANGE x 3 | x 3 | x 3 | x 3 |
| SPRINTS: | SPRINTS: | SPRINTS: | SPRINTS: |
| 3 x 4 x 30m<br>30 secs REST<br>2–3 mins BREAK | 3 x 4 x 30m<br>20 secs REST<br>2–3 mins BREAK | 3 x 4 x 30m<br>30 secs REST<br>2–3 mins BREAK | 3 x 4 x 30m<br>30 secs REST<br>2–3 mins BREAK |

## KEY TO EXERCISES

### Drills

**Knees:**  fast and high knee action, short steps. Hands behind back with rest of body relaxed.

**Flicks:**  fast kick-backs, heel to buttocks. Hands behind back, rest of body relaxed as it advances.

**Speed:**  legs as in the knee drill. Add a fast arm action. Elbows high on the backswing, hands up to shoulder level on the forward motion. Fingers relaxed.

## Knees

## Flicks

## Speed

## Bounding

**Double Leg**:  feet together, bunny hop forward, with full arm swing. Land on ball of feet first and repeat with as much power as possible in each jump.

Double Leg

1    2    3

Speed Hops

1    2    3    4

**Speed Hops:** a more upright double leg bound but at the top of the jump, bring your knees to your chest with power.

**Jump Sprint:** jump two-footed from box and land on the balls of both feet. Immediately sprint forward as fast as you can.

Jump Sprint

1

2

3

4

### Skill

**Drives:** sprint hard, drive off back foot and keep shoulde
and head low for 10–15 metres. Gradually allow shoulders to
come up.

### Ins and Outs:

Smoothly accelerate and decelerate between sprinting and
jogging.

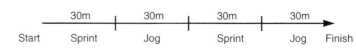

### Gear Change:

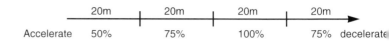

Pick up speed at each marker.

### IN-SEASON SPRINTING – SERVICING

Choose any one of the sessions from weeks 5–12 and
include it in your weekly programme for servicing. Experiment
– make up your own.

**Note: do not sprint-train if you have injured joints – it will
aggravate them.**

### FINE TUNING SPRINTING – POWER/SPEED

Follow the routine opposite for a three-week period to fine
tune your speed. This regime is suitable for all sportspeople
at whatever level. **Do not compromise quality for quantity.**

| MONDAY | TUESDAY | WEDNESDAY | THURSDAY | FRIDAY | SATURDAY | SUNDAY |
|---|---|---|---|---|---|---|
| **SPEED TRAINING** | | **SPEED TRAINING** | | R E S T | G A M E | **FLEXIBILITY** |
| **STRENGTH TRAINING** | **CLUB TRAINING** | **STRENGTH TRAINING** | **CLUB TRAINING** | | | **EASY AEROBIC EXERCISE** |
| CIRCUIT TRAINING | | CIRCUIT TRAINING | | | | e.g. Swim, Cycle, Run |

# CHAPTER 11

# FLEXIBILITY

I often wonder what all the fuss is about concernin
stretching and flexibility. It sometimes seems that the fastes
players have the shortest hamstrings and every rugby playe
worth his salt has a stiff lower back and neck! On the othe
hand, every gymnast, dancer or swimmer can get int
positions that defy belief – yet they all get injured. Why
Perhaps because too much flexibility is as bad as too little i
sportspeople. What is flexibility?

---

**FLEXIBILITY**

The range of movement in a specific joint, or over a few joints
working together. Assuming that the joint is not damaged and the
ligaments are intact, then the **length of the muscles** that cross the
joint or joints usually determines the range of movement.

---

There is probably an optimum level of flexibility for a joint c
set of joints – and probably for the type of sport you play.

Too much movement may cause the joint to be a b
wobbly or unstable in certain conditions. This hypermobilit
may be as big a problem as hypomobility or stiffness tha
restricts movement and puts stress on soft tissues such a
muscle, tendon or ligaments.

So why bother with stretching exercises? A certain amour
of flexibility is needed to perform skilled movement
efficiently, such as running, throwing or serving in tennis.
more important reason for stretching is to reduce th
likelihood of injury. A long, strong muscle can resist strai
imposed on it during training and games.

**Stretching** before activity will help 'loosen' muscles and so
tissue, help you to psych up for the game, and after th
activity help reduce muscle soreness. This type of stretchin

Colin Jackson - flexibility personified.

s not likely to produce a more flexible sportsperson. **Flexibility training** – or developmental stretching – as an organised training session will lead to longer-term benefits of improved ranges of movement.

The only difference we note between warm-up/cool-down stretches and flexibility sessions are the length of time for which the stretch is held.

| | |
|---|---|
| Warm-up/Cool-down stretch: | hold for 14–15 seconds. |
| Flexibility stretch: | hold for 20–24 seconds. |

The routine shown below can be used as part of the warm-up/cool-down at each training session or game session or as a flexibility training programme. It is a general programme suitable for all sportspeople.

Note: **Warm up** – run or jog for at least five minutes before stretching.

**Do not bounce** – smoothly apply the stretch up to the limit – focus on the stretch – hold and then release.

**Breathe easy** – don't hold your breath – breathe smoothly during stretch.

**Repeat** – each stretch to be performed at least twice.

## LOWER BACK

- Push Backs
- Knee Squeeze
- Crucifix
- Push Backs

## UPPER LIMB

- Shoulder/Triceps (Back of Arms)
- Shoulder/Biceps (Front of Arms)

## LOWER LIMB

- Gastrocnemius (Calf)
- Soleus (Calf)
- Iliopsoas (Groin)
- Adductor (Groin)
- Hamstrings
- Quadriceps

## NECK

- Rotation
- Side Bend

**Remember ... warm-up first, and for warm-up/cool-down stretch, hold it for 14–15 seconds, for a flexibility exercise hold it for at least 20–24 seconds.**

## LOWER BACK

Push Backs

Knee Squeeze

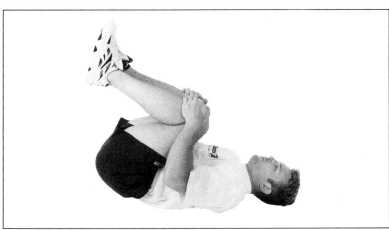

Crucifix

## LOWER LIMB

Gastrocnemius
(Calf)

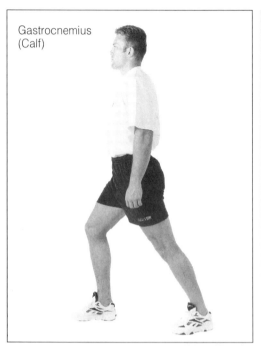

Soleus (Calf)

Iliopsoas
(Groin)

Adductor (Groin)

## Hamstrings

## Quadriceps

## UPPER LIMB

Shoulder/Triceps (Back of Arms)

Shoulder/Biceps (Front of Arms)

## NECK

Rotation

Side Bend

# CHAPTER 12

# HIGH PERFORMANCE FUEL

'You are what you eat' is a popular phrase. Do you look like a 'tub of lard' or a 'lean mean-fighting machine'? You may appear all right on the outside – but what about the inside? Are those arteries clogged up with fat?

It is generally accepted that a healthy diet is:

- **low** in fat (especially saturated fat), salt and sugar and
- **high** in fibre-rich starchy foods, with plenty of fluid, especially water, and the ideal amount of vitamins and minerals.

Why is healthy food so boring? It isn't – or at least it doesn't have to be. So long as the diet supplies the right amount of energy and nutrients to keep you healthy and allow you to train, then you can select from a vast range of foods and drinks.

Your diet should provide the correct proportion of:

- **carbohydrate**
- **fat**
- **protein**
- **vitamins and minerals**

as well as fibre and water.

There is no such thing as 'good food' and 'bad food'. The nutritional benefit depends on the amount of it you eat and how often. Check out the guidelines overleaf.

## NUTRITION & PERFORMANCE

Muscles need energy to work. The particular source of energy our muscles use is called **glycogen**. This is produced by the liver from carbohydrate foods and it is stored in both the liver and muscle tissue. You *must* therefore make sure that while you are training hard you are getting enough carbohydrate to replenish the glycogen stores and avoid fatigue.

**Note: Eat After Training – it can take up to two days for your muscles to refuel with glycogen after heavy training. This process can be speeded up by eating a carbohydrate snack such as sandwiches, bananas, cereal bars or dried fruit within two hours of finishing training. Regular carbohydrate snacks – four to five during the day – will help.**

Muscles, when trained, can also get energy from the breakdown of **fat stores** into fatty acids. By using a mixture of glycogen and fatty acids as fuel the body can make its glycogen stores last longer. Glycogen is spared and performance can be maintained for longer. This is particularly important in activities that last longer than 60 to 80 minutes, as a reduction in glycogen is the main limiting factor of performance, causing fatigue.

**Short Burst Activity:** high intensity exercise (anaerobic) such as sprinting and circuit training uses carbohydrate as the main fuel – only this fuel source can provide energy quickly enough.

**Longer Duration Activity:** lower intensity exercise (aerobic) such as distance running or cycling uses a mixture of both carbohydrate and fat. The utilisation of fat, though, takes a long time so some carbohydrate is always burnt up.

**As you get fitter and better conditioned your body will utilise fat more quickly and in greater proportions. This will allow you to perform longer – and keep thinner. Have you ever seen a fat marathon runner or Tour de France cyclist?**

## WHAT FOOD DO WE NEED?

A quick look at the pyramid below will help you understand more about the types of foods you need and the sort of amounts.

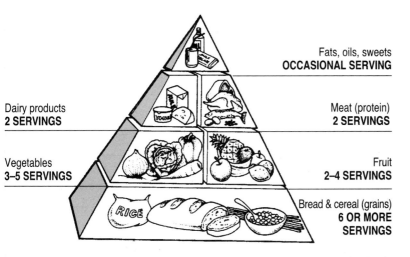

Larger quantities are at the base – including most of the carbohydrate foods – while the apex holds the smaller amounts of fat, oil and sweets – the stuff that you really shouldn't eat a lot of.

Don't eat too much from each group, get the proportion right and try to eat a varied diet. It will be so much more enjoyable.

### Carbohydrates

As already mentioned, these are a vital part of the diet if you are in heavy training. They should make up 50–70% of the daily calorie intake. Foodstuffs include:

- **Bread and cereals:** bread, preferably wholemeal, oatcakes, breakfast cereal.

- **Rice, pasta and potatoes:** brown rice if possible, and baked potatoes in preference to 'fatty' chips. All types of pasta and noodles.

- **Biscuits:** wholemeal, bran or cereal bar types.

Starchy food makes the basis of all meals. It was commonly thought that this type of food was fattening. That is only the case if it is smothered in fat to cook it or butter to eat it.

### Protein

You do not need vast amounts of protein in your diet – even if you are weight training. Any excess will be simply stored as fat, not turned into muscle. Daily intake should be approximately 1–1.5 grams of protein per kilogram of bodyweight per day. A high-protein diet will not increase your strength – only a strength-training programme with a well balanced diet will do that. Foodstuffs include:

- **Meat, Poultry, Fish:** beware fatty meat.
- **Fish:** avoid fish in oil.
- **Peas, beans, lentils, soya beans:** all kinds of pulses are high in protein and low in fat.
- **Dairy Products:** most are high in fat so try semi-skimmed milk, reduced-fat cheese, low-fat yoghurt.
- **Eggs**

Vegetarians must be careful to vary their protein food sources. This is because proteins are made up of amino acids. Essential amino acids, of which there are eight, cannot be made within the body and must be obtained within the diet. Foodstuff may contain some, but not all, the essential amino acids, so a mixture of food must be taken, usually including dairy products and eggs.

### Fat

Fat is a concentrated source of energy. Unfortunately it is not easily utilised and too much fat in the diet leads to weight gain as the fat is stored as adipose tissue beneath the skin. If you could readily use the fat stored in your body, you would probably have enough energy to run from John-o'-Groats to Land's End – no problem! We need some fat in our diets to provide essential fatty acids and fat soluble vitamins needed for healthy bodily functions. *But*, generally we eat too much fat. That is because it is usually the tasty bit, e.g chips and cream cakes. Two main types of fat exist:

- **Saturated:** mainly of animal origin and tend to be solid at room temperature, e.g. butter, cream and animal fat. *Should be avoided* as they tend to raise cholesterol levels.
- **Unsaturated:** mainly of vegetable and plant origin and

tend to be liquid or oils at room temperature, e.g. sunflower oil, polyunsaturate margarine. *Should be used only in moderation.*

**Note: Try to eat less fatty food and try to make it the *unsaturated type* if at all possible. Fat should account for only 30–35% of your daily calorie intake.**

*Ways of Reducing Fat Intake:*

- Don't eat fried food – poach, roast, grill, boil, steam or bake instead.

- Use low fat/reduced fat alternatives – that is semi-skimmed milk or polyunsaturated margarine for example.

- Avoid pastries, crisps, cream cakes, mayonnaise and sweets.

- Eat white meat and fish instead of red meat or fish in oil.

**Vitamins and Minerals**

If you are eating a varied diet which includes plenty of fresh fruit and vegetables, wholemeal bread and cereals, then you should be getting your full complement of vitamins and minerals. If you are not sure, take a multi-vitamin tablet each day.

**Note: salt in too great quantities is not good for your blood pressure. You do not need to add salt to meals – there is enough in the food anyhow.**

**Drinks**

If you are dehydrated before or during training, your performance will suffer. Water is an essential part of your diet and is important to almost all the body's functions. You should drink between two and four pints of water a day – more if you are training hard.

**Remember – if you feel thirsty you are probably already dehydrated.**

During exercise your body loses not only water but electrolytes, which are substances such as sodium, potassium, chloride and magnesium. Available on the market today are many so-called electrolyte drinks which include these substances. These may be a very tasty or an absolutely repulsive alternative to water. I prefer plain water.

Some drinks contain glucose of sugar or carbohydrate and are used to hydrate and give the body extra energy during exercise.

### Training and Drinking
Remember:

- Drink before you are thirsty.
- Drink small amounts regularly before and during exercise.
- Rehydrate after training.
- If your urine is clear and copious, you are probably okay. If it is dark, thick and in short supply you are probably dehydrated.

**Alcohol is a diuretic and can cause you to lose fluid and lead to dehydration. Don't drink the night before training or playing.**

### Eating for Competition
Before you play you need virtually full energy stores. Eat well the two days leading up to the game. If anything, load up the amount of carbohydrate you eat.

You don't want a full stomach to play on, so your last meal should be light and taken 3–4 hours before the competition. Make sure you are hydrated.

During competition, keep hydrated by taking on fluid at irregular intervals. If you are working hard for 60 minutes or more, some carbohydrate would not go amiss – such as a banana or a carbohydrate-based drink.

**Note: do not eat a sugary snack prior to performing. It will not help. In fact it may well reduce your energy level.**

### GOLDEN RULES

1. Eat regular meals.
2. Drink at least 2–4 pints of water daily.
3. Eat plenty of carbohydrate-rich foods to build up your energy stores.
4. Always refuel within an hour after training.

5. Have a rest day to allow the body's energy stores to recover and rebuild.

6. Reduce the amount of fat in your diet.

7. Vitamins and mineral supplements are generally unnecessary.

8. An enjoyable and healthy diet is one that includes a variety of food.

9. Everything in moderation.

## BREAKFAST, LIGHT MEALS AND MAIN MEALS

The suggested meals below are some of our favourites. They are high-carbohydrate, low-fat but tasty alternatives.

---

### BREAKFASTS

$1/_2$ grapefruit or I oz cereal with semi-skimmed milk
2 slices toast with jam or marmalade
Tea or coffee with semi-skimmed milk

2 rashers grilled lean bacon
1 grilled tomato
1 slice toast
Tea or coffee with semi-skimmed milk

---

### LIGHT MEALS

1 jacket potato with various fillings, e.g. low-fat cottage cheese, baked beans, coleslaw, tuna and sweetcorn.

Wholemeal sandwiches with various fillings, e.g. low-fat spreads, tuna, crab, salad, or chicken.

Pasta mixed with low-calorie mayonnaise and tuna or other low-fat options.

## MAIN MEALS

### Tuna Pasta (Serves 2)

1 onion
1 tin plum tomatoes
2 level tablespoons tomato purée
1 pint stock made from chicken stock cube
6 oz pasta shells
7 oz can tuna fish
Salt and pepper
Olive oil

Chop onion and fry in a little olive oil in a large frying pan or wok until soft.

Chop tomatoes, and add with juice to the onion, together with the stock, tomato purée and seasoning and bring to the boil.

Add the pasta and simmer until the pasta is cooked (approx. 15 minutes).

Remove from heat and add the drained tuna fish, flaking it gently without breaking it up too much.

### Chicken Hawaiian (Serves 2)

2 skinless chicken breasts
1 oz Cheddar cheese
2 pineapple rings
4 rashers smoked bacon

Heat oven to 200°C, 400°F or gas mark 6.

Place a pineapple ring on each chicken breast and sprinkle with the grated cheese. Wrap each breast with two rashers of bacon.

Bake in oven on a baking tray for 25–30 minutes.

Serve with jacket potatoes and fresh vegetables.

### Mushroom Macaroni Cheese (Serves 2)

6 oz wholewheat macaroni (or other pasta can substitute)
6 oz mushrooms
1 onion
4–6 oz Cheddar cheese
1 tin Campbell's condensed mushroom soup
Black pepper
$\frac{1}{2}$ teaspoon dried mixed herbs
Butter

Heat oven to 200°C, 400°F or gas mark 6.

Boil macaroni in water for 10 minutes (or as recommended on packet).

Meanwhile, chop onion and fry in butter in a large frying pan or wok until soft, then add sliced mushroom and cook for 5 minutes.

Add soup (undiluted) and mix well. Season with black pepper and mixed herbs.

Drain macaroni and add to soup mixture, mix well. Add grated cheese and mix again.

Turn into a greased ovenproof dish, bake in oven for 25–30 minutes until the top is lightly browned.

# CHAPTER 13

# BREAKDOWNS

Occasionally some of the pain you may experience while training is not just the effort, but caused by injury.

**GOLDEN RULES**

1. Do not train on an injury
2. Apply first aid
3. If no improvement, ask for advice

A player's worst nightmare.

Remember you are training hard and subjecting your body to force beyond its normal expectation. Overuse injuries are as common as traumatic ones.

**If you are feeling tired – mentally or physically – or sore, with extreme muscle or joint tenderness, then take a few days off training or reduce the intensity of your training and have an easy week.**

There is no problem – and in fact some people would argue that it is a benefit, in having an easy week in terms of training, every third or fourth week. Beware the dreaded burn-out.

We will deal here with soft-tissue injuries, i.e. not bony, those that should not require you to visit the doctor immediately.

Consider the following:

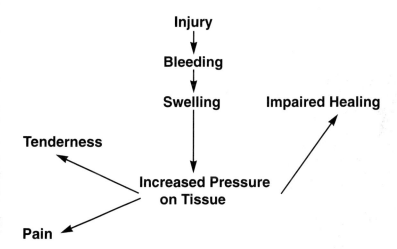

If treatment is started *immediately*, the time to full recovery of acute soft-tissue injury can be shortened considerably. **So act straight away!**

I recommend the P.R.I.C.E. procedure, before a doctor is involved:

**P: Protect**   Take the strain off the injured area by use of a crutch, sling, etc.

**R: Rest**   No activity for a few days

**I: Ice**   Apply ice packs for 20–30 minutes regularly to the area

**C: Compress**   Apply a compression bandage, e.g. Tubigrip

**E: Elevate**     If possible, sit with the injury held at above heart level

If significant improvement does not occur in three to four days, then consult your doctor or friendly physiotherapist.

Mental attitude and meticulous organisation can play an important part in recovery from serious injury, as the former Olympic 400-metre runner Derek Redmond makes clear:

There are two factors which enabled me to keep on training injury after injury and make a comeback to top international athletics. These were self belief and a training method taught to me by a sports physiologist, which made the long struggle back to the top easier to cope with mentally. I called this 'Taking Care of Basics', but more about this later.

When I ran my best time ever way back in 1987 in the semi-final of the World Championships, all I was doing was qualifying for the final the next day. In fact, during the race, I spent a lot of the time actually looking around and I even slowed up over the last 50 metres. However, I still managed to run in 44.50 seconds, which at the time was a British record. But I still knew that I could run much faster even though I never ran a good final from that day on. This knowledge that I could do better was one of the points I focused on during training, as well as the obvious aim: Olympic glory.

'Taking Care of Basics' was taught to me at a time when I had difficulty focusing on training. I was going through a stage after my fourth or fifth Achilles operation (I have had ten operations now!) in 1991 where I couldn't be bothered to train because I felt that the mountain was just too high to climb (the mountain being the 1992 Olympic Games). My physiologist had the great idea of breaking down my training aims into three stages:

Stage One:    the basics ... all the ingredients that make up my complete training programme e.g. weights, track work, diet, flexibility, physio treatment, sleep etc.
Stage Two:    achieving a time we felt it would take to win the Games.
Stage Three:  Olympic Gold

If I had control over all the elements in Stage One and took care of each one, then I would stand a good chance of making the time it would take to win the Games. If I made the time, then I would stand a good chance of winning the race – in this case the Olympics. But although I had some control over making the time, I had no control over winning the Games, as I might run in 43 seconds whilst someone else could come along and run in 42 seconds.

Keeping this in mind, I could take the pressure off my self by not thinking about the whole mountain, but instead concentrating on the basics. All I could do was take care of these and let the other two stages take care of themselves.

As odd as this may seem, this method really helped me to cope with the next three to four operations as well as the long road back to recovery and competition.

## COMMON INJURIES ASSOCIATED WITH TRAINING

| COMPLAINT | PREVENTION AND TREATMENT ADVICE |
|---|---|
| **Achilles Tendinitis:** Tenderness in the area between the calf and the heel. | Warm up and stretch thoroughly. Rest until pain diminishes. Consult a doctor if pain persists. |
| **Delayed Muscle Soreness:** Soreness that occurs one or two days post-exercise. | Warm up well before exercise and stretch after exercise. Train at low intensity for a couple of days. |
| **Groin Strain:** Pain or tightness inside upper thigh pain on leg swing. | Perform adductor muscle stretches gently and rest for 3–4 days. Warm up sufficiently before running. |
| **Hamstring Strain:** Soreness or pulling at the back of the leg. | Prevent by good hamstring stretch and warm-up. If very sore, refrain from vigorous activity for at least two weeks. Can take up to six weeks to recover. |
| **Runner's Knee:** Pain or tenderness over the outside of the knee and just above and below. | Avoid high-intensity running. Check running shoes are not worn or unevenly wearing out. May need to see about orthotics in your shoes to correct running action. |
| **Policeman's Heel:** Pain under the heel and sometimes along the arch of the foot. | Check running shoes – do they offer enough support? Stretch calf muscle regularly and rest until not too painful. |
| **Low Back Pain:** Pain across base of back. | Strengthen abdominals and perform back stretches regularly. Supplement stretches with extra hamstring, quadriceps and hip stretches. Rest until full range of movement returns. |
| **Shin Splints:** Tenderness along inside of lower shins. | Warm up gradually. If painful, stop, rest and apply ice. If pain persists you may need to see a doctor or physiotherapist. |
| **Tennis Elbow:** Pain on the outside of the elbow, particularly when gripping. | Grip-strengthening exercises when no pain is present. Stop exercises that require strong gripping, such as pull-ups. Apply an ice pack regularly. |
| **Shoulder Pain:** Pain in the shoulder joint when lifting the arm above the head. | Stop weight-lifting and contact practices until a full range of pain-free movement returns. Then begin strength-training exercises. If the shoulder looks at all deformed contact a doctor immediately. |